About the Author:

Stuart Wilde has written fifteen books on consciousness and awareness. His perceptive and quirky way of writing has won him a loyal readership over the years. He has also had a big effect on the New Age and the movement for a greater awareness; they were all fine 'til Stuie rocked up! Over a period of twenty years he came to be known as 'the teacher's teacher' because of the influence he has had on other writers and lecturers in the field. Stuie Wilde started making predictions about fifteen years ago. He goes into trance and tells you what will happen later. The weird thing about Stuie's predictions is that they almost all come true, sooner or later. You can follow them if you like at www.stuartwilde.com.

BY
STUART WILDE

The titles above, with the exception of Wilde Unplugged: a Dictionary of
Life, are available through Hay House Publishing—www.hayhouse.com

God's Gladiators

BY
Stuart Wilde

Published and distributed by:

Brookemark LLC
P.O. Box 4368
Chattanooga, TN 37405 USA
www.brookemarkllc.com
ISBN 0-9714396-3-X

Edited by: Rachel Eldred
Cover and book design: cd

First Edition
10   9   8   7   6   5   4   3   2   1

Printed in the United States of America

Contents

I

Morphing Walls, Spiritual Slavery, and So On

After years of trying, the veil between this world and the next lifted. At first, the walls in my home started to morph from solid to fluid, and then I saw the eternity of creation beyond the concreteness of our earthly existence. Naturally, I wondered if I was imagining it all. But others close to me began to see the same phenomena and after a hundred such experiences, I started to become more and more convinced. Then, one day, in August 2000, in New Orleans, I went through the wall of my hotel. After that I had no more doubts.

I'm not quite sure how I did it. I wasn't intending to go through the wall. At first, it morphed from solid to hazy, then it went soapy looking and I suddenly found myself pulled through to the other side. I thought I had been gone only a few minutes, but once I got back to my room I realized the bedside clock had ticked through 50 minutes of Earth time. There is no real time, of course, beyond the earth plane—everything is eternal. So are you. Eternity, it seems, is what exists between atoms and molecules.

Since then, I have had many very strange experiences: beings morphing in and out of my perception, some human looking, some not; walls that bend and wobble; the strange unexplained scents of flowers; flashes of light; and doorways, endless doorways. All around us are worlds more intricate than you can ever imagine. There is dark and light. The tales we have been told of the spirit worlds and the afterlife are vaguely true in part, yet wildly inaccurate in other aspects. What follows are some of the things I've seen, presented within the confines of my comprehension.

Teachings about reincarnation that say we live one life after the next over eons, suffering pain and confusion until we eventually reach God and nirvana, are not really true. I think reincarnation is probably just a spooky idea invented to stall you. To ensure you don't become confident enough to search for the truth. God is right here, not at the end of a journey. You are at the center of everything. There is nowhere to go. You are already there. Reincarnation is celestially geographic. Creation is a hologram. It is everywhere. You are everywhere. Everything and everyone that ever lived is inside you: Hitler, Mother Teresa, Genghis Khan, the greatest creators, the saints, the animal worlds, the plant kingdoms, and so on. They are all within you and you are inside them. You are every thing that ever lived. The Kingdom of God is within you.

Scientists say our universe is made up of trillions upon trillions of particles. They are not exactly correct. There are only a very few basic particles (three, I think, and the antiparticles perhaps) and they are everywhere, which gives the illusion that there are many trillions in every square inch of reality. But in truth it's a hologram of the same three particles. When a scientist smashes a particle in an accelerator he is in fact smashing what seems like a particle to him, but it's just a hologram. He can't smash the real particle, it's not there. The holographic universe is minutely small and enormously large at the same time.

The three forces of nature, electromagnetic energy, nuclear weak, and nuclear strong, are not really separate energies; they join together not only in the solid world but in the eternal world, too. Gravity doesn't belong to these three forces, which is why it resists researcher's attempts to unify it with the others. Gravity is a symmetry of the three basic particles, a geometry inherent to the three particles. It is not a separate force. It's a shape that comes from the basic particles and it belongs only in the solid 3-D world. Gravity is a factor of the intrinsic nature of the particles that make up our solidity. Once you 'rotate up' to the other dimensions there is no solidity and gravity ceases to exist. The contemporary idea that our 3-D reality rotates up to ten dimensions and on to 26 dimensions is correct. What happens after that, if anything, I can't say. I've seen a mirror world, which looks to me like it may be a part of the 26 dimensions. The mirror world may just be the antiparticle world, but maybe not. I just don't know as yet (reality turns itself inside out and outside in, through 26 dimensions, trillions of times per split second. The outside-version is the mirror world.) We humans are inside out in this dimension. (See chapter 13 in my book Sixth Sense for a fuller explanation of this.)

So in the non-solid world, gravity obviously doesn't exist and once our 3-D solidity morphs, you could drop a billiard ball on the floor and it would go straight through it. Time is what makes solidity solid to our perception. Once time began, solidity gradually appeared. We perceive solidity not just because atoms oscillate quickly to create solidity, but also because the mind moves forward in time. Your mind moving forward in time is what makes a wall hard. Thinking is linked to solidity. Once you stop your mind, the wall will start to morph after about 20 seconds or so.

In the non-solid world, things are pulled together by their intrinsic 'feeling'—the force of attraction. Gravity is a 3-D version of this intrinsic feeling. Love attracts, hatred repels. Gravity is the geometry of love in our 3-D universe. And as I've said, the three other forces: electromagnetic energy, nuclear weak, and nuclear strong, are all one. They belong together in a higher dimension, beyond 3-D, even though we experience them in our 3-D world. They are part of eternity. This is why all the mathematics of the Unified Theory extends to infinity; and this anomaly confuses researchers into thinking they are wrong. They have found the answer, but they don't see it—infinity is the answer. Join the three forces of nature, sideline gravity because it doesn't exist at a higher level, and there you have the beginnings of a theory. There's a bit missing, i.e. there are four forces but gravity isn't one of them—but never mind that for now. Just remember gravity is down here, it's obvious really. You can't rotate it up to another dimension any more than you can rotate a mountain into the air. It's weird that scientists haven't seen that. It's self-evident if you don't get too complicated.

The teachings about yin and yang are not totally correct either. There is no such thing at a higher dimension in the hologram. Duality is an illusion. There is no separate 'masculinity' or 'femininity.' They are two geographies; aspects of the same thing. The multi-dimensional solid and non-solid universe is intrinsically feminine. Masculinity is part of her sadness. In order for creation to come about, she had to distance a part of herself. The idea that woman came from Adam's rib is round backwards; as are most of the things you've been taught. Masculinity separated from her (Eve), not the other way round. There is a dedication in masculinity that most don't see. It is the utter loneliness and sadness of being seemingly disconnected from the feminine whole. But this disconnection is only temporary, an illusion. In the hologram, masculinity is joined to all things. The warrior's final destiny is to grant himself absolution, purify himself, and return to her—the Goddess. She, who is the multi-dimensional universe.

The teachings about God and the afterlife are simplistic to the extreme. They are a terrible trap invented to control you. I'll talk about that later. Life is a trap. We live, as I have said in my other books, in a prison created by our minds and for our minds. In the olden days, it was called the Reflective Sphere (the Sphere). It's everywhere. It is deep inside all our religious teachings and our New Age philosophies—it is in every spiritual practice that was ever invented. The stuff you think is holy and good, the very ideas and practices you think elevate you to the status of the Chosen One (he who will be saved and risen up), is a trick, one that ridicules and belittles your sacredness by trapping you even deeper in the prison of the Sphere—the prison of your mind.

SORRY, SORRY,
LOVE ME, LOVE ME.

Once you see it, you will throw up. Before you see it, you will get angry and not believe me. The idea of the Chosen One is a lie invented to control people. It's also the mind's way of deluding itself.

How do you know God is spiritual? You don't know. You never questioned it. You are so totally manipulated you probably believed that you can't even question the idea—it's against 'the law'. What is the law? Bullshit—rules of control; barbed wire for your mind.

The Sphere tricks you mercilessly. It's very callous. God is not spiritual, not in the holy way you conceive 'spiritual' to be. God can't be spiritual, for if it were, it would have to become special. Special is an idea the ego invented to feel more secure. It's the way the ego traps and torments you. God is not insecure, so It doesn't need to be special. God can't be special. It is magnificent beyond words, but It is humble and It is everywhere. There is no 'spiritual,' not in our ridiculous sense of the word. The idea of God's 'spirituality' is just another con fed to you by the fat controllers of this world to hold you back. It's how they keep you in their prison.

Your ego, being scared at times, probably bought the concept of God's spirituality to elevate its self-importance. It's sad. It's a mistake. It's an idea used to ensure that you never get close to the real world—to the real truth. God's spirituality is a presumption you accepted to ensure you never had to go through the fright of seeing or comprehending the real thing. It's part of your mind's defense. It's a condom. One that ensures you are never infected by the truth, for if you were, your world would collapse. It's a struggle for us to sustain the illusion of our perception of the world, our lives and our reality; it takes effort and causes pain, but that is less odious for many than the psychological and spiritual unraveling that occurs once you see the true nature of creation.

Once you see God you will know it is more than a white light and you will also know that all our spiritual teachings are designed to enslave us. You probably knew it all along. Maybe, like me, you were too scared at first to admit it. It was too horrifying. But years of transdimensional terror cured me. I became brave. I eventually stood my ground. I was lucky. I nearly died.

The world is lying to you. Quickly throw this book away if you want to believe the lies, for the next few pages will unravel what you think you know. In truth, there is nothing to hold on to. Let go. Or stay in prison and try to become a Chosen One. It will doom your soul to lower and lower oscillations, and you will eventually fall so far you will never escape.

Ninety-five percent of the people on this planet are already irrevocably trapped in the freezing cold world of ego, illusion, importance, power, and materialism. The other five percent are being led gradually to the same fate. The trick is unbelievably clever. It is so total, so complete. It's all around you as a diamond- shaped net in the etheric. On Earth it's a massive all-encompassing control trip, exercised by the political, social, and financial forces of control. All the sources of information you have are inside the Sphere. It's the accepted propaganda. It takes you to their place, the spiritual dungeon of their reality, an insidious world. They feed off you. On the ground, your money is stolen and your activity entrapped. You are a slave to control and greed. The transdimensionals in nearby etheric dimensions also trap you and feed from you. A bit like in the way it's explained in the film The Matrix; similar but not exactly. Your etheric energy is fed off, entrapping the essence of what you are, while your life force is sucked from you. If you sleep more than about three to four hours a night you can be sure you are being drained. It's sinister and there is very little you can do to stop it, partly because you don't know how to, and partly because you can't move past your fear. The transdimensionals can walk through walls and haul you off or tear you apart, and no amount of naïve incantations to the light and to God, or any other bits of misinformation you might labor under will save you. The illusion of this power is so total, few are brave enough to resist.

But all is not lost. In this book, I will show you why it is not lost. I will talk to you about our protectors—God's Gladiators, as I call them. They are real. They are human. They are split evenly between men and women. They are very courageous and exquisitely beautiful. They are very secret. They work without pay or recognition. They work to ensure that humans can escape if they wish to. They are being helped from beyond by Inner Gladiators, as I call them, but the help is not in the way you'd imagine. Forget what you know. It's been filtered down to you surreptitiously to confuse and frighten you; to make sure your never have the tools to make an end-run for freedom. Remember, almost everything you have been taught is round backwards. Heaven is warm and hell is cold—trust me, I've seen both of them. You can work it out for yourself, love is warm, hate is cold—easy-peasy-lemon-squeezy, and you wonder why no one has noticed.

People think this is an end-time, that the known world will end very soon. Many New Agers are gearing up for December 2012 as that marks the end of the

Mayan calendar. Where are the Mayans? Extinct—tut, tut. Their world ended rather sooner than they expected. Clue? What were the Mayans infamous for? It's not in the travel brochures. They were infamous for throwing innocent victims off high walls—lots of them, tens of thousands of them. What happened to the Mayans? Ding! Ding! The forces of retribution don't piss about. Don't buy December 2012, it's a trick.

Let's go, if you can stand it. It takes enormous courage to leap to freedom. And here's the scary bit. No one can save you, not me or any other, not any philosophy or practice. You have to save yourself. Anyone who claims they can save you is an agent of the Sphere. As you attempt to leave its influence, they use every trick they know to make you turn back. They control everything and right now, they control you, totally. They control you without you even knowing it. What you think is personal freedom is a mind game designed to keep you in your place—to keep you as a slave.

2

The Matrix

Confused? Watch the film The Matrix again and again. I've seen it 56 times so far. There are hundreds of symbols in the film. How they got there, I don't know. It's irrelevant. It's all there albeit as an allegory.

The hero, Neo, dies in room 303. Thirty-three is the number of the initiate. Zero is the feminine principle—eternity. So 303 is the initiate embracing eternity. Neo's bedroom, where he hacks away on his computer, is room 101. Eleven is the number of the master builder. So early on in the film, Neo is the master builder working around eternity. Look at the silver, chalice-type cup on Rhineheart's desk. Notice the gold lining of Neo and Mr. Smith's jackets—El Dorado, the golden one; the initiate who doesn't know he is an initiate. When Neo goes into replication he is covered in mercury. They inject the same fluid into Morpheus' neck. Mercury is the alchemic fire.

Neo wears a plum red blanket as he climbs the stairs to meet the crew of the Nebuchadnezzar. Why plum red? Watch the large rabbits on the television behind the Indigo kids—what do they mean? Listen to the Oracle; she talks about the true nature of fate, free will, and time. Look for one of God's Gladiators. He's pretending to be blind. He nods when Morpheus and Neo walk out of the elevator.

Did you see the number three? It appears many times, especially in the railway station where the last fights take place. Look at the graffiti to the right of Neo as Mr. Smith throws him up against the wall. What does it say? Shadow. Whose shadow? Are Neo and Mr. Smith one and the same?

The Matrix is the story of the Holy Trinity. Morpheus is God the father. Neo is the son. He is referred to as Jesus several times in the film, though the reference is masked. The female character Trinity is the divine goddess, Mary Magdalene, the feminine principle that was excluded from our Holy Trinity by the male writers of Christian dogma. The Christian idea of the Holy Ghost is a concoction—misinformation used to disempower the female's rightful place at the top of the trinity. There is no Holy Ghost. Ghosts are the astral image of dead people. The idea is pure drivel.

The Matrix tells the time-old story of the death and the resurrection of the initiate.

The filmmaker's rendition of the Matrix as green symbols that tumble down the computer screen is a fairly good effort. Though the real thing doesn't drop in straight lines as digits on a screen, and it flows horizontally as well as vertically. Though it drifts from the ceiling downward it does travel upwards—but only in rare situations. Most of it travels diagonally across your vision in lines or groups of lines that form bands several inches wide. In parts, the real thing moves much faster than in the film, though in other parts it travels much slower. There is no overall uniform steady speed. In the morph of solidity, past the Matrix, are vortexes of energy that lead to other dimensions. The bending walls at the end of the film, after Neo stops the incoming bullets, are very accurate.

What does it all mean? It means that something up there loves us and is trying to get us to open our eyes and see for the first time. When Neo is told about the nature of the Matrix and the invisible control over humanity, he throws up. The Sentinels exist in our world, and are on the side of the controllers, but I've never seen any that look like those in the film. The fields upon fields that contain the pods where humans are grown are not accurate. But the idea that we are energy that is used to sustain this evolution, as well as other evolutions, is very accurate.

It's all there in the film. Goodness knows how it got there. From deep inside the filmmakers' souls I'd imagine, where all things exist as one. Someone, somewhere is talking about the demise of the Matrix and our escape. The key to the film is at the end after Neo has been shot. Trinity breathes over him and she says, "I am not afraid anymore... so you see, you can't be dead, you can't be, because I love you. You hear me? I love you." Then she kisses him and says, "Now get up." It's the most beautiful scene in the film. It's where the love of the Goddess revives the comatose God. She resurrects the wounded male (the ego) and kisses him, bringing him back to life. The ability is in her selflessness. It's part of her compassion, her eternal kindness. Males can do the same when they stand inside the feminine spirit that is within them.

The resurrection is the same for you as it is for Neo in the film. Once you are no longer scared, the forces of control can't feed off you. The hold over you and your life breaks down. Watch The Matrix even if you have seen it before. It's all in there, at least in a rudimentary form.

3

Free Will is for Amateurs

Here are some of the things I've learned. Some are frightful, others are beautiful. Many, at first, are hard to believe. I'm not trying to convince you, or win you over. I'm only telling you what I know. I'll tell you the easy stuff first.

We come from an incredible place; sadly our return is not guaranteed. There is a war on, you know? Many deny it. It suits them to.

In the film Stigmata, an ancient Nag Hammadi scroll known as the gospel of St. Thomas is quoted: "The Kingdom of God is inside you and all around you, not in buildings of wood and stone. Split a piece of wood and I am there. Lift up the stone and you will find me. These are the hidden sayings that the living Jesus spoke. Whoever discovers the meaning of these sayings will not taste death."

You can't get there with your mind.
(Sorry, sorry, love me, love me.)
That is the impossible riddle.
It's in your heart
and beyond that.
It's past your death.
But there is no life
and so no death.
This is a dream.
We are
not really
here.

For those of you who yearn to return to your true spiritual home, I have some wonderful news. You are home. You are at the center of everything. It's under your nose. All that stands between you and the incredible magnificence of it all is the mind. You can enter via physical death or you come from a mental death. A mental death feels like what I'd imagine a physical death would feel like. It requires you to voluntarily let go. Many physical deaths are not voluntary. Once your body quits you are stuck, you can't change anything. Pre-death is preferred.

SHE-SHE-LA-LA

She-She-La-La is a feminine god. She's very scary. I fell in love. She showed me how to die. I was frightened. She asked me to surrender, whispering, saying, "There is no life and no death." I eventually agreed with her. She held my hand. I'm not worthy of her. She showed me the warrior's way to die—then bliss, the bliss of resurrection. I could have gone much sooner. She's patient. She-She-La-La is my eternity. I am her.

✦ ✦ ✦ ✦ ✦

We are not here. It's all a farce, an illusion. While we labor under the misconception of our physicality, we are trapped. Once you see that you are immortal, you are free. It requires a rotation of the mind, a bit like turning a pillowcase inside out. Do you remember Necker's cube from one of my previous books? See it below.

Diagram 1:
Necker's
Cube

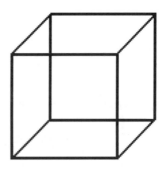

Imagine you are a dot in the back corner. If you pull that corner toward you, the cube turns inside out. Suddenly, the dot is free from the confines of the cube. I discovered on my travels that it is the mind pushing forward in time from one thought to the next that makes your body and the surrounding world seem solid. Once you stop the mind, the cube turns inside out, and the solid world begins to morph and become fluid. This reality has at least two states: inside the cube (solid, in prison) and its mirror opposite outside the cube (not solid, eternal).

Free Will
is for Amateurs

If I told you the secret to this human evolution is very simple, many would not believe me. The mind likes complexity. It's how it controls you. The worst Nazi in the world is your mind. The Nazis of World War II were our shadow externalized and made horrifically real. Each of the Nazis' victims was killed in part by their own shadow. It's hard to comprehend as we are entwined and bound by ideas of right and wrong, good and evil. We need right and wrong so we can feel special. As a victim you imagine that you have rights; compensation is due. You expect to stand elevated and special in the eyes of others, who will hopefully commiserate and assist you through your pain. The cult of the victim is a commercial business. It's the outcropping of our need for easy money, attention, and glamour.

The mind and your identity within it, the ego, is no different: it also wants control and attention. It will never let you out of its prison. It cons you into thinking it knows. Usually what it thinks it knows is misinformation, offered as ludicrous ideas—it's the mind's guessing game. When the mind moves from guessing to action, we call it free will. Free will was invented to create confusion. It's the way the Sphere ensures that escaping prisoners make little or no headway.

Free will is sold to us as vital and special and all-important. Vast tomes are dedicated to it. It's spoon-fed to you as something you can't do without. The idea of free will is cleverly cloaked to hide its lethal characteristics, knowing it will appeal to your ego's need for specialness; playing to your need to be separate and individual. The idea is tap-tapped into your mind as a woodpecker taps a tree. You are offered free will as a pillar in the human rights' edifice; something to be defended and to die for. It's placed sneakily in the American national identity, "...land of the free [will]." Welcome to the invisible prison of the Sphere. The prison you probably insist is not there.

Free will is for amateurs. It got you the job you hate, the rotten relationship you endure/d; it got you to the stoplight just in time to hit the school bus, which you thought was an accident, but was the mind driving you, in time for a disaster. It carried you lurching from one rotten choice to the next. Sometimes, rarely, it got it right, well almost right, but most of the time it brought you the pain of restriction and suffocation, confusion and boredom. You suffered the exhaustion of the slavery it imposed on you, then you got angry and protested, so it said, "Okay, move to California, try that." Perhaps you did move. But within a few months, after the novelty had wore off, down came the asbestos fire blanket of your mind and its free will. You found yourself, yet again, in a sunny prison with other prisoners who are crawling along in traffic in the lane next to you.

Let go of free will. It's a con game, a very clever one. It's the very best of reverse psychology. Tell people to fight for free will, tell them how important it is. In this way you glue the idea to their arrogance and their need for identity. Then once the idea hardens and is accepted, sit back and watch people give over to it. Watch the pitiful sight of prisoners dying to defend the camp guards who stand over them in the watchtower. The subtlety of the manipulation is unbelievable. Almost no one has seen it. Some have intuited its existence, but they are ridiculed into silence. And very few know how to rotate out of the snare it uses to capture the mind, disallowing real information and personal truth. This reality is a zoo.

FEELINGS, EMOTIONS, AND SENSATIONS

I've previously written about feelings, emotions, and sensations, so I'll keep it very brief. Sensations are binary electrical signals that travel to your brain to indicate what is happening in your environment, touch, for example. Emotions are reactions in your etheric to the mind's options and ideas. All emotion is housed in the etheric. We say, "My heart is heavy today... my dog died." Of course your heart is the same weight as it was yesterday. It can't feel sad; it's a muscle. It's the emotional reaction in your etheric that creates the sadness, and in this instance it is the etheric over the center of your chest that has reacted.

So it is natural that people see emotions as being of the heart. Emotions are not true information. They are just the outcroppings of some opinion you hold. Only feelings are real. Feelings come from inner knowing. They are extra sensory perception (ESP).

Mind is the camp commandant, your personal fat controller. Sensations are the camp's telephone system. Emotions are the theater performance the prisoner is required to attend every day, like it or not. Feelings are God's Gladiators calling faintly from the distance, reassuring you that the camp guards have no real bullets and that the gate is wide open. Of course, it's hard to hear the Gladiators calling, as the theater noise is deafening and when that is not in full swing, the camp commandant is barking new orders. The camp's loudspeaker system (the media) floods you with misinformation that tells you how dangerous it is to make a run for freedom. It sells you on ideas that feed the ego to trap you. It sells you constant fear. It cons you into thinking that what is happening to others in the world is somehow a part of your imminent journey. It sells you on the need to search for security, and it says that the camp and its overall fat controllers will keep you safe, here's your welfare check. It also repeats over and over again that the fat controllers are very important. Here is the news, "The Speaker of the House of Representatives said today..." Who gives a fuck what he said? It isn't going to help you anyway. "Israeli soldiers shot and killed three Palestinians today." So, what's new? They kill Palestinians every day and the Palestinians try to kill them when they can. If you are not Israeli or Palestinian, or in some way connected to those who were shot, what is it to do with you? You might commiserate out of human compassion, but it's not your responsibility. Anyway, there is nothing you can do about it. It's not as if you can pop over to Jerusalem and bang a few Arab and Israeli skulls together, and say, "Stop this bullshit or else."

The point of 'news' is to drip feed you fear and to offer you endless problems you can't fix. The idea is to generate a steady stream of helplessness, ensuring that you accept the idea that you are powerless—that the fat controllers know best. It ensures that you buy the idea that someone important is running the show, someone you must defer to and respect. Of course, politics is nothing more than an externalization of your mind and its desire to control you and those around you to make it feel safer. Give away the TV, ignore the papers and you are already walking toward the gate.

There is a plan, a divine plan. It's your alternative incarnation after you have had enough of free will, the mind and the zoo we are in. The plan rests in your subtle feelings (not in your emotions) and it comes bit by bit, as you need it. It is splendid. It's more than you can ever imagine.

PUT THIS ON YOUR FRIDGE IF IT FEELS RIGHT:
"I HAVE NO PLAN.
I MAKE MINUTE-BY-MINUTE
MY DIVINE PLAN."

Now, don't confuse a divine plan with religious ideals about conquering the Earth for Jesus or Islam or whoever wants to be the next fat controller. Don't get confused with your ego's domination and its desires for your life. The divine plan will not necessarily bring the ego the things it craves: attention, money, glamour, and recognition. More likely, it will ask you to serve and be selfless, and it will require you to accept and follow along in blind faith. It will often test you to see if you are for real. It will demand instant action. Just as you are lying down on your bed after 20 hours non-stop, it will say, "Get up and go call Brother George in Denver and make sure he's okay and following the plan."

You will probably argue at first and go to sleep instead, and the plan will say, "What a wimp, she's hopeless. It's a waste of time messing with her." Then it drifts away from your subtle feeling as it can't be bothered with you and you are lost for a while. Next, free will seizes the opportunity to make a come back in your life and suddenly you are driving 17 hours non-stop to Steamboat Springs for no reason at all other than to run away.

The divine plan is not like a Nazi-style control trip, as God, by Its very nature, can't be a controller like your mind can; God has to allow things to be free. Control is demonic. The Law of Allowing, as some call it, requires us to accept evil and good, error and correct judgment. That is why there is pain and what we mislabel as 'evil' in our world. If God is good, how can it allow evil we ask? It has to. It is the ultimate liberator. It can't control.

When people talk about the will of God they are selling you the gobbledygook of the Sphere. There is no will of God. Just the outcropping of what God is, love. Unconditional love liberates and lets us go. It allows without personal criticism or judgment. It allows even when what is happening is not the personal choice of the mind.

Cᴏɴᴛʀᴏʟ
ᴀɴᴅ Aᴅᴍɪɴɪꜱᴛʀᴀᴛɪᴏɴ

Administration is hiring enough competent drivers to run the trains on time. The drivers can choose to drive the trains under your terms or not. Control is different from administration. It's the imposition of your will on others. It is demonic. The fat controller of your mind decides to impose itself, intimidating some, cajoling others, attempting to control everything: how people look, what they eat, where they go, how they pray, who they have sex with, what they ought to do. Meanwhile, it steals their money (energy) under the guise that each should contribute to the greater good. Doing so, it feeds off the energy of others, enslaving them to its demands using guilt, regulation, manipulation, and/or threat.

To give away the need to control is the first step in the divine plan. First, you stop dominating and attempting to control your life, you then offer the same escape from torment to those close to you. If you have children, you can learn to administer their lives rather than terrorize and dominate them. The divine plan states that there is no plan. We are trying to let go and arrive at a place where things arise spontaneously from our collective joy of being in the presence of God.

+ + + + +

The Goddess energy is just about to arrive in our world if she has not already done so by the time you read this book. She will hurt the male-dominated world and will give the fat controllers a fright. She is both the destroyer and the eventual resurrection. The terrible lies of the world will be exposed. We are all pretending. We pretend we have the interests of others at heart. We pretend to be generous. We pretend to love using our mind, not our heart. We pretend to care, it grants us self-importance. We pretend to be truthful and yet we have never listened to the truth within and we lie like crazy all the time. We play Mr. Nice Guy and yet we are often mean and rotten to people. All who are very dark within play the Mr. Nice Guy game. It's part of their propaganda. When you see a Mr. or Ms. Nice Guy watch very, very carefully. The 'Nice Guy' often hides a fat controller, a manipulator of the worst kind. I've chased after a few black magicians in my time—only when they got in my way though. I never saw one who wasn't hiding behind his or her 'Nice Guy' image. Very few people are openly rotten.

The world is going to change. The tyrannical fat controller will be fatally wounded. The house of cards will collapse. The time is now. The game is up. The forces of retribution are just about to march into Babylon... should be interesting.

4

THE VISION OF THE
DAWN TRADER

I was shown a vision. It was set several hundred
years ago. A sea-going clipper was making headway in
a rolling sea. Some of the crew were on deck tending to
their duties. Below deck was the captain. He was rather
overweight. He lay in his bed masturbating; beside him
was an empty bottle of port. On the deck below were
hundreds of Africans: men, women, and small children
in chains. The clipper was a slave trader. The prisoner's
misery drifted through the vision as a sickening black
cloud laced with the groans, the smell, the feces, and the
filth. The women and some of the men were being taken
by the crew on a daily basis to satisfy sexual needs. There

was little or no food. Some of the Africans were dead, chained beside others who lay on the deck still alive.

Another ship appeared on the horizon. Let us call it the Dawn Trader. The crew of the slaver warned the captain. He took no notice and remained in bed. When the other ship got closer, the crew could see it was flying the Portuguese flag. It didn't bother them at first, but as the Dawn Trader closed in on them they became more and more nervous, and when it was less than 100 yards away, the Portuguese flag came down and up went the Jolly Roger, the skull and crossbones. There is nothing very jolly about the Jolly Roger. In the middle Ages, it was the naval battle flag of the Knights Templar; pirates only later adopted it. The Knights Templar were part of the forces of retribution in their day, until they became corrupt and they were arrested and slaughtered under the orders of a French king whose name slips my mind right now.

Grappling-hooks struck the gunnels of the slave trader and it could no longer escape. The crew was slaughtered and the captain was tortured and killed. The Portuguese took the African prisoners and threw them in the water to wash them, some who couldn't swim drowned. The rest were hoisted aboard the Portuguese boat. The slaver was looted and burned. Then, something amazing happened. The captain of the Portuguese boat ordered it to turn around. Then he and his crew sailed

600 miles back to the coast of Africa. The captain set the prisoners free, warning them that they would never get another chance. "Keep away from the white man," he said. He added that they should be especially careful of their own people. You see, the local Africans were the ones who captured villagers selling them to both black and white slave traders. The blacks ran the slave trade in Africa. Did you know that? They did so for thousands of years before the white man showed up—a point that is conveniently left out of history books. All that Roots, Kunta Kinte stuff sounds good to Hollywood, but it is not quite the whole story. Slavery is an African business. It always has been. The Africans were the wholesaler; the whites were just another retailer among many. The African has always been his own worst tormentor— he still is today.

The people who run the world, who control and print the money, those who seem to have all the power, only think they control the world. God controls the world by not controlling it. Meanwhile, the Sacred Mother, the Goddess, keeps order like any good mother might. She sometimes comes as a miracle, healing with unconditional love, a love that descends as a strange silence that is sometimes accompanied by the scent of flowers. When she does come in, it causes an unusual pressure on your ears. Sometimes she comes as a whack in the head. On a long enough timeline, the Dawn Trader always shows up.

31

Evolution seeks its own balance. This world is far too precious for the rotten eggs who run the world to be allowed to actually run it. They serve their purpose. Because God is everything, so the devil is also part of God. In fact, if you think about it, the devil is handy; he works for God, keeping a steady stream of the faithful heading back to a more righteous path.

5

STUIE AND THE LADY OF THE LAKE

After Brother Stuie got pissed off with lecturing, not long after he was banned from pretty much everywhere, he starts pondering what to do next. So off he goes drinking and dancing and causing trouble to keep himself amused. Meanwhile, God talks to his deep inner soul: "Stuie, you scallywag, stop fighting and drinking, and stop all this sex and romance BS, it's hurting you brother, go find the Lady of the Lake and study with her a bit." Stuie knew a bit about life in the inner worlds, as he'd been fighting the transdimensional Greys for a couple of years, but he knew diddlysquat about goddesses or ladies of the lake.

Anyway, Stuie trots off to a remote lake looking for the Bodhisattva Kuan-Yin—he wanted to see if she'd bonk him. That, of course, was Stuie's male ego talking. At the time he was upset at not being allowed to fight and/or go after an Irish girl who at the time was the love of his life.

Trying to bonk the Bodhisattva Kuan-Yin would be silly beyond words and very dangerous. But Stuie fancied himself to be a Jack-the-Lad. He'd always go after the most impossible lady in the room: the Mafioso's wife, the six-foot-six supermodel, the lesbian with the hair lip, and the timid lass in the corner—the virginal looking one in the corner who's twiddling with her frock right now. Stuie nearly got himself killed so many times, cos his subtle and brazen manner quite often worked. He'd be with the Mafioso's wife behind the statue of Apollo in the garden, when coitus interruptus would creep in—barking dogs. Stuie was over the wall and back round the front door, dry cleaned of any sins, as fast as you could say, "Pass the wine." "Sorry, sorry, love me, love me," Stuie would then say to anyone who would listen. Whereupon he'd slug back a red wine or two and try his hand at the bimbo from LA, or someone else. "It's all mathematics," Stuie would say. "The center of the universe is a fractal. It is feminine and complex and beautiful and magnificent and terrible beyond words. As long as you can see everything as an infinite fractal it cannot resist you, especially if you are not just pretending to love people but you actually mean it at the time."

"Jot that down," he would say, as he often did a hundred times a week. "Jot that down."

Now, on the way to the lake, Stuie stops off for a quick drink. It's Dublin, at 1:45am, and Stuie shows up at a club off Grafton street where the manager recognizes our lad, whisks him up to the VIP lounge, and sits him down in a comfy chair next to Tom Jones, who is sitting there with what seems to Stuie like an etheric hard-on that says, "Do any of you girlies wanna play Delilah avec moi?" Stuie isn't too keen on this Tom Jones bullshit, as our lad is trying to be more feminine and show up at the lake with a good demeanor tattooed on his heart.

An empty chair is next to Stuie and Stuie asks the universe at large, who this chair is for. The universe says, "Wait here Stuie, there is someone about to show up." An hour or so later, David R. walks out of the elevator and the manager of the VIP lounge walks up to him and says, "Stuie Wilde is waiting for you, please come in and sit down." What was amazing about that was, Stuie had not told the manager that he was waiting for anyone, and how she knew that David R. knew Stuie was a mystery. (In fact, the universe told her, and of course young David spooks out a bit wondering how it's done and why everyone seems to know his every move.)

Seated next to Stuie he says, "Stuie, for over ten years you have been very influential in my life, and you keep creeping in from time to time as if you are influencing me and my destiny." Stuie smiles and says, "Whaddayawanna drink?" Then Stuie tells David that David is a fuckwit and a wimp and that his world will probably fall apart, and that he will never become anything really serious until he agrees to fall apart and hit rock bottom; or, go for plan B where he quits being David and follows Stuie to the lake, which, unfortunately for David, he was not prepared to do at that time.

After Stuie had finished with David, there were a few lingering thoughts about fighting and shagging in his mind, so he thinks he'd better redeem himself in the eyes of God. He walks down to the dance floor and while dancing hits every single person in the club—hundreds and hundreds—etherically, one after the next. He brushes past their souls telling them, "Let's evolve, stop being a prat, evolve—come to the light."

Stuie is now knackered so he goes home to bed and dreams a few impossible dreams as any would-be Jack-the-Lad might. Of course, at that time in our Earth's evolution there was a steady stream of people trying to bash or wound Stuie, so a few of Stuie's dreams were spooky nightmares.

Stuie gets up in time for a hearty Irish breakfast and because he had moved beyond free will, his mind was liberated from the need to work things out, so he continued on his journey to the lake. On the way there, he met a very beautiful Welsh witch. She had green eyes and very black hair. She held Stuie's hand tenderly and said, "You are the most beautiful man I have ever met. I have waited 37 years for you." Of course, to Stuie's male ego that was pure bliss. A rendezvous was set up. But Stuie became very frightened. He thought she was part of some terrible trick. It all looked too easy. Stuie had advisors. Women. Visionaries. So he calls one up and says, "I'm scared. Can you work out what this witch is all about? I think it might be a trick." The visionary says, "She's here to teach you something about Avalon that you won't understand. It's part of the Lady of the Lake, the hidden feminine spirit. Trust her and follow her as far as needs be." Needs be turned out to be four days. Then Stuie continues on his way to the lake.

Stuie decides to stop off at a healing temple along the way. He felt grubby and too masculine. He washes himself and puts oils and exotic spices in his hair. Next, he puts on colorful silks, several silver bracelets, and the most beautiful silver necklace you have ever seen. He knew the Lady of the Lake, the one who gave King Arthur his sword, was called Argante. He knew that some thought her name derived from the French for silver, argente. He then prayed and fasted for nine days, took colonics, and drank green slime, which he'd been told is very good for you. Now he felt ready. He went to the lake and waited. Eventually, three young women dressed in pre-Raphaelite clothes traveled across the lake in a boat. It was broad daylight. It reminded Stuie of a painting he saw at the Tate Gallery in London. A young man rowed the boat.

One of the women gave Stuie a bottle. In it was a potion. Stuie thanked her and drank it. He then went into the fairy worlds for a bit where he met his shadow: it frightened him. Meanwhile, there was no sign of the Lady of the Lake. He was a bit disappointed. But he had by now opened his heart and rested his soul, which was all part of his greater journey to find her. But he didn't know that at the time.

Brother Stuie knows wizards and shamans. After the incident at the lake, he dropped in on one of them to see if he knew how to entice the lady out of the lake. The wizard, who was quite young for one of his ilk, said something very strange, "Stuie, can you love the devil. Could you ever love the devil?" Stuie was a bit taken aback as he'd been raised a Christian, and even though he didn't care much for religious organizations, he preferred to stay on the white, brighter side of things and give the devil the golden elbow.

"No," said his mate the wiz. "Unless you can love the devil, you will never find Argante, the Lady of the Lake. For if you did, she would reflect to you your unprocessed dark side and you would be terrified and run." Stuie knew the brother was right. So he stored his silks, jewelry, and bottles of exotic spices in the roof of an old barn in southern England and he made ready to head off to look for the devil to tell him he loved him. By now, Stuie had figured out that all the devil needs is attention. If even one person loves the devil unconditionally, without judgment or criticism, then things might improve. Stuie knew that the devil sought redemption as we all do. Yet, Stuie still hadn't figured out back then that the devil is a kind of gladiator working for God, scaring wimps into righteousness. Stuie hadn't quite grasped the awesome truth that light and dark are on the same side—God's side.

Bare with me, if you will, I think you'll find the next bit rather interesting, for Stuie was seriously up for giving this devil business a go. He had spent a while punching it out with the sky people and their UFOs. He was well aware of what an entity coming through your bedroom wall at four in the morning feels like. He also knew what it was like to be hauled off against your will to be rooted up the bum while some grim transdimensional, devoid of any comedy, stuffs a little gizmo up your nose. You see, Brother Stuie had already graduated from the University of Pure Terror, so the devil did not seem to be quite an impossible challenge as one might at first imagine. Stuie suddenly realized that all the horror of his time with the sky people, the Greys, and so on was part of his training. It was part of the process of meeting the devil to tell him he loved him.

So off he trots to meet the devil, when something completely bizarre happens. He was sitting in the garden of the old barn where he had stored his stuff, when his arm went translucent. It felt hot. It was an inner heat, a kind of celestial sunburn. It lasted for about two hours. At dawn, two days later, Brother Stuie woke to find his whole body had become light. The heat was terrible. It totally incapacitated the fellow and he soon became a gibbering wreck, unable to tend to his day-to-day needs. The heat almost never ceased and Stuie couldn't sleep while it raged. He was awake for 23 hours a day. The heat came out of his hands, his feet, his eyes, and his right shoulder was always boiling hot. He stuck an acupuncture needle in his hand hoping to redirect the heat but nothing happened, except little bolts of blue light, like lightning, flew off the needle.

Ya man, Stuie was doing it tough. At times he would lie on the stone floor in agony for hours unable to move or even make it to the toilet; he would lie in his urine. Just below his navel flowed, what he described as, a column of etheric energy that he experienced as pure terror. Stuie said it was an ancient fear. He thought perhaps it might have been the fear and abandonment he had experienced in childhood. During the heat, Stuie would do eight hours of fear and then two hours of abandonment, then he'd be allowed to rest for an hour and he'd drift into sadness. Grief for his life, grief for the world's pain, grief for the animals, grief for the seeming futility of life on Earth—the sadness, tears, and anger that comes from not being able to fix the world's problems. Stuie finally figured out that sadness and joy are one and the same.

The agony lasted for months. At first, Stuie resisted it. The pain was too terrible. But after a while, he let go and accepted sadness for what it was. The more he accepted the pain, the shorter and shorter the periods of agony became. But the heat never subsided. It just became more manageable. By now Stuie had given up on the Lady of the Lake and his idea of meeting with the devil was miles from his mind. Survival was the only game in town.

It was during all this that Stuie started to see the morphing walls. All manner of bizarre experiences occurred. One day, a video film appeared mysteriously on the wall of a room. There was no equipment or projector. A hazy screen suddenly appeared, hovering on a blank white wall. It jerked around a bit as if slightly unstable. A film of a cat in a forest played. The film started off in black and white and gradually moved to light sepia colors. Not like the bright Technicolor we see in films, just images lightly dusted with color. While the film played it tugged uncomfortable at Stuie's navel.

He watched the film with a pal of his. It lasted 45 minutes and had no soundtrack. What was even more amazing was his friend, an English women in her late 30s, watched a completely different film simultaneously on the same section of wall. Her film was about the industrial revolution and the women's Land Army, which was part of the Dig for Victory campaign in Britain during the war.

Stuie was now beginning to wonder. He suddenly sees that this celestial heat might be more than just a strange internal phenomenon. Of course, in those days, Brother Stuie was still wondering if perhaps he'd gone mad. But the video rather convinced him that he had not. Later on, six of his close friends also acquired the heat. Stuie felt for their pain, but in a way he was pleased that they had gotten the heat, as now he was no longer the only weirdo in town.

Meanwhile, spooky characters in grey cars started following Stuie about, helicopters hovered over the barn, and military men showed up at Stuie's seminars, pretending. When he went to America that year, he was photographed from a distance all the time, and he would smile for the camera and love the military men unconditionally; one started crying and Stuie loved him all the more. Stuie never could figure out what they wanted with him as it's not like our man Stuie is a revolutionary. He doesn't even know who's in government. When Yeltzin retired, Stuie didn't find out for three months. He came to believe that the sky people and some of the folk on the ground are in cahoots. Who's running the show, wonders Stuie?

Of course, Stuie didn't give a fuck who was running the show, cos he knew God was running it—he'd been out there and seen it. Furthermore, Stuie figured that whoever felt they were running the show should continue to do so. It was not natural for him to want to run anything, it has never been his way. And anyway, he was off to find the devil.

Finding the devil is a lot harder than you think, for the devil is very slippery and he hides in people's hearts. To look for a fellow in Southern England with cloven hooves and a spiked tail, carrying a pitchfork is a bit of a silly ploy. So, Stuie enlisted the help of his female visionaries. Stuie is a scamp, but he deeply respects women, and all his advisors, except one, are women, and for a while he even had women bodyguards when things got dangerous. Amazonian girls, totally lethal—Stuie loved them especially.

The visionaries tell Stuie that the only way to find the devil is in the inner worlds. They said that the devil doesn't really exist, though there are many entities that share the devil's identity. So in a way, he does exist and in a way he doesn't. Stuie soon got pissed off with the technicalities of finding the devil, so he went to a gothic

S&M bar frequented by black magicians. He was hoping
for a lead. The owners of the bar got very angry with our
lad and wanted to chuck him out of the bar. But Stuie
stood his ground and spooked them so badly they backed
off. He was with Brother Paul at the time, and Paul is a
very soft and kind man who can take ya fuckin' head off.
Having Paul there convinced the S&M crowd that this
was one fight they were bound to lose. Though they did
chuck out a few of Stuie's other pals.

Anyway, in the bar Stuie met a magician of the
satanic, left-hand path who was dressed in black as a
priest. Stuie thought that quite appropriate, as there's a
lot of black magicians at the center of the Catholic
Church in Rome. Stuie globed a molecule of his identity
on to the black priest's back and followed him about
(etherically) for a few days, hoping to find the devil. It
didn't exactly work but it gave Stuie a clue. Whenever he
thought about the black priest, he'd imagine taking the
black-hearted fellow back to God.

It was a great ploy. You see, Stuie was trying to
entice the devil, as there is no way the devil would allow
that S&M phony priest back to God. Now something
quite terrifying happened. Stuie had been talking on a
syndicated radio show in America over the phone about
what a load of bollocks the power of the UFOs is—that
they don't have any tricks we don't have. (Stuie believes
in UFOs, cos he's seen over a hundred of 'em, and the

Greys were coming through his walls for about 18 months. He says they are all bullshit, a control trip to con you into thinking they are a higher consciousness from another star system.)

Anyway, after the call to the radio station, an entity with claws comes up behind Stuie and tries to rip his crown chakra off. (Now if your crown chakra comes off you are dead.) Stuie spins round and the entity backs off. Stuie was sick for days. But he decided that the devil had better come up with a better move or quit, as Stuie felt the devil had wasted his best shot.

+ + + + +

You can search and search for something and never find it, then when you give up and sit down, suddenly it's there. Well, with Stuie and the devil it was exactly that scenario. Stuie was in another world of sorts, looking for answers when suddenly a scary looking character, that Stuie imagined the devil might look like, showed up and stood in front of him, brazen as anything. Zombies were with him/her/it—they were like the living dead, all bones and strange skulls. They came up and threatened Stuie, and at first he was on his guard and didn't react, but suddenly one got very close, inches away, and Stuie gave him a soft but firm whack in the head. Soft, but firm? What's that? Well, that's how Stuie described it, soft but firm. The zombie was shocked, as it was used to people being scared of it; suddenly things had gone a little pear-shaped in the zombie world. About ten more showed up to try their hand and Stuie gave them the same 'whack in the head, howdy-doo-dy' greeting. Then, a whole bunch showed up; but they had seen what had happened to the others and soon backed off—they realized that ya man Stuie might be a part of the Dawn Trader. Whoops.

Meanwhile, the devil-type character slinked off, none too sure. But by now it was all too late as Stuie had seen him and now Stuie reckons he could find him anytime. Meanwhile, some 'contrails' appeared overhead. Contrails are those vapor-like trails in the sky that are laid out by white unidentified military planes the government knows nothing about. They are supposed to contain pathogens. Stuie doesn't know what a pathogen is, but he knows when he sees a contrail and that they make you sick. It's all part of the up-and-coming flu epidemic, so they say, which is supposed to thin out populations and make things easier to control. Ninety percent of all contrails are over America, the other 10 percent are supposed to be over Brother Stuie. The contrails and the devil aren't far apart. So Stuie thinks anyway. (Doesn't it irritate you when people pretend to protect you, yet they are really trying to kill you? Lies, lies, and more damned lies.)

Anyway, Stuie had just gotten over the zombies when the contrail appears overhead. He raises his hand and says in a very loud voice, "No." The contrail pops like a soap bubble and disappears. Now Stuie is very confused. Was it real or not? Stuie tries his hand at another one about a week later, and it pops the same way. Stuie starts wondering if the UFO scallywags in their flying machines aren't doing the contrails just to scare people—is it all but a ploy to keep people frightened so there is more etheric food? In the end, he reckons it's a bit of both, real and not real. Stuie is absolutely convinced, however, that the UFOs and the darker part of the 'hidden government' are one and the same thing—part of the devil's plan to control everything. It's amazing what you find out when you look for the devil.

For a while Stuie was a bit depressed, as he didn't like the idea of millions of people dying of some epidemic. He got over it. Anyway, help was not far off. But Stuie did mention, as he trotted off, that one should do everything one can to boost one's immune system as that might be the difference between toppling over and keeping upright. "Toppling over can get on your nerves," says Stuie. Jot that down.

When looking for the devil, so he could find the Lady of the Lake, Stuie started wondering who the fuck was controlling everything. He'd ask awkward questions like who owns the Federal Reserve? And why are

American workers dying of stress to pay private bankers
for money that never existed yesterday, money on which
the ink is still wet? Money that their own government
could print and dish out interest free, thus liberating all
Americans from a terrible crime. Hundreds of thousands
drop dead every year. Never mind the old holocaust, this
is bigger—it exterminates drip by drip by drip. What a
con. Never mind the Afro-American slavery of the past;
it's sad of course, but not as sad as modern slavery, which
has already taken out more people than the holocaust
ever did—Americans of all races and creeds, bless their
slightly naive souls. Stuie was crying one day, crying
about people's heinous traits, when he came to the
conclusion that the Federal Reserve and the Nazis are the
same outfit. Though, according to Stuie, the Nazis had
nicer uniforms. (Stuie has never been too keen on the
Nazis but he likes their uniforms.)

Anyway, Stuie couldn't mess with the Federal
Reserve, as that is not his department; but he did mention
one night in a Sydney bar, when he was a bit sloshed, that
once the Goddess shows up, sleazy ol' Mr. Greedscam
and the Federal Reserve had better learn to swim.
Skolling another Lemon Ruski, Stuie added that
Wall Street wasn't far behind the Federal Reserve in
crimes against humanity, and that the best investment
on Wall Street was some obscure outfit called
waterwings.splash.splash.com.dot pass the net.

So Stuie is still searching for the devil while he's trying to find out who owns the Western media. "Whoops," says Brother Stuie. Now he doesn't think there is a conspiracy, but the disinformation is so prevalent and so similar that Stuie reckons the media owners and the transdimensionals are of like mind. Stuie even said that the transdimensionals feed ideas to the fat controllers to make the world a lousier place. He says you don't need reptilians walking around in sheep's clothing; it's easy to feed any fat controller's mind, they will buy anything that offers them power over others. That's why the media likes to frighten people—it gives the illusion of control and it helps them believe that they are special and immortal. "Propaganda ain't proper," says Stuie.

BROTHER STUIE SAYS,
"LET GO OF BEING SPECIAL.
IT'S A TRAP.
IT'S PART OF THEIR CONTROL MECHANISM,
AS IS SUGAR.
LET GO OF SUGAR. IT MAKES YOU DOCILE."

YEAST IS IN BREAD AND BEER.
THE TWO CHEAPEST THINGS
YOU CAN BUY ARE BREAD AND BEER.

49

THEY ALMOST GIVE THE STUFF AWAY.
Ding! Ding!
STUIE WARNS PEOPLE AGAINST BEER.
HE SAYS,
"YOU DON'T DRINK BEER YOU ONLY RENT IT.
FIVE MINUTES LATER
YOU ARE IN THE REST ROOM
GIVING IT BACK."

YEAST FEEDS OFF SUGAR.
IT BLOOMS IN YOUR GUT, ENTERS YOUR
BLOODSTREAM AND ROBS YOUR ENERGY.
IT'S JUST ANOTHER
FEDERAL RESERVE-TYPE ENTITY
FEEDING OFF YOU.
TAX AND SUGAR ARE THE SAME,
ACCORDING TO STUIE.

While looking for the devil, Stuie observed all the
mechanisms of wealth and he discovered a strange thing:
anything valuable seems to have a monopoly on it. The
same few people sustain the monopolies for generations.
The gold price is fixed every morning in London by a few
lads who work for the same outfit that seems to own a
chunk of the Federal Reserve. Diamonds is another closed
and rigged market. The same devil-like characters start

showing up everywhere. Stuie says, "You don't have to look far to find the anti-Christ."

Anyway, Stuie was not looking for the anti-Christ, he was still out looking for the devil and Stuie's not into gold or diamonds—he's sold on the value of silver as he knows he can entice Argante, the Lady of the Lake, with silver. Well, he hopes he can. Who am I kidding; you know Stuie got her in the end.

I was going to stop here, but I suppose I ought to tell you how he did it, otherwise you might feel ripped off and sad and creating more sadness is against Stuie's religion. We're trying for the other side of sadness—joy.

To cut the story short, I'll leave out some of the minor details and get to the bit where Stuie found the devil. Stuie wouldn't tell me exactly how he did it; he said that it was a bit too dangerous to disclose exact details. Yet he did say, "Imagine it like this, if you will." (I like the way he says, "If you will." It's nice to know there is an escape clause.)

Stuie said that the devil is too big a job for any one entity to handle. So it has been handed out to many, and they all form part of the forces of control and darkness. Some are transdimensional, pretending to be from elsewhere in the universe, and then there are their partners on the ground: aerial Nazis and "Ground Control to Major Tom" basically. Stuie says they are all rinky-dink once you are not scared and once you can love unconditionally. "Practice loving Saddam Hussein," says Stuie. Stuie is quite good at loving people he doesn't like, though he thinks Greedscam and the Federal Reserve are a large dollop of heinous crap and he hasn't quite been able to digest and love them. Stuie reckons if he waits long enough, the Dawn Trader will get 'em, and he won't have to love them. I told him that was avoidance and denial, and he looked a bit sheepish and said, "I ain't perfect."

After Stuie had looked at the monopolies and lies of the world, and after he had discovered who owned these monopolies, he went back to his job of finding the devil, or as many as he could find, given that the devil is in loads of different spots at the same time.

Stuie decided that if he was going to tackle the devil, he'd do well to have a more certain grip on God and God's will. Of course, Stuie knew God didn't have a will. But he reckoned God would have an intrinsic loveliness that might be confused with will. Stuie had a fair inkling what that loveliness was but he had to make sure.

He went to a forest and stayed in a temple. There he went through a mini-death. On the other side of the mini-death was God. It's not like the way you think it is. It's bigger. So Stuie says, "Forget all that living in the light stuff, God's a lot more than a lovely light or some heavenly dimension."

When Stuie saw what humans call God, he was very disappointed. He was out some place in the cosmos looking back at Earth and there was this huge oval-shaped orange football—bit like the NFL ball but longer, a lot longer, like several hundred miles long. The totality of what humans think God is only came to an orange ball of emotion a few hundred miles across! It was fairly transparent and Stuie spent time amusing himself looking through God back at Earth. Stuie said it was like looking through the back of God's head. He found it a bit embarrassing. Stuie wasn't up for disturbing the orange ball. Of course, the orange ball isn't the real God; just the totality of what humans think is the real God. Our lad said, "It was sad that humans didn't have a fuckin' clue." Stuie can be a bit direct at times, but he usually knows what he's talking about.

Anyway, Stuie eventually got through to where the Celestial Higher Authorities (the Authorities) ponder the fate of the world. He wondered if that was where the Dawn Trader gets its marching orders. It turns out that it is more complicated than that. Inside every molecule of every Nazi on Earth, and elsewhere, there is a self-destruct button with the picture of a ship on it. Just kidding. Usually, the Nazi presses their own self-destruct button; but if they are still dithering in their illusions, the Forces of Retribution press the button for them. So the Dawn Trader turns out to be an externalization of the dark. It is a part of the dark side—a vacuum cleaner designed by God to make sure none of the rats get away with it for too long. It's amazing what you find out when searching for the devil so you can kiss him on the lips and tell him you love him. You see, the light is not allowed to attack the dark, so it made sure the dark would destroy itself over a long enough timeline. It's a hidden virus in the dark's system. Stuie says, "Jot that down. There is no escape—dark cell death, bloody amazing."

After Stuie found that out he clicked his heels with joy. He realized he didn't have to do anything and nor did anyone else. The dark ones of our world are already imploding deep within and it will soon manifest on the surface. But Stuie did wonder if there were any vacancies in the Forces of Retribution for a willing beginner. Pressing buttons seemed to Stuie a fun game while whiling away the hours before the pub opened.

Now ol' Stuie is fairly fast on his feet perception-wise, but when dealing with the Authorities he slips into his 'it's humble to stumble' mode real quick—he wasn't up for a cosmic whack in the head. The Authorities said, "Stuie what have you been up to?"

The Authorities sometimes reminded Stuie of the fuzz, perpetually asking questions they already knew the answers to. Anyway, Stuie stumbled through the story of the Lady of the Lake: silver, spices in ya hair, blah, blah, and so forth, then he waited. "What else?" asked the Higher Beings. "Well," said Stuie, going into defensive mode, "I know I'm a bit of a scallywag, but I took it upon myself to talk to people about ducking out of the slammer the modern Nazis have constructed for their minds. Is that okay?" Stuie didn't wait for an answer; he knew the Authorities weren't into control so the answer was obvious. He went on to explain that all he ever did was talk to folk. Sure he spooked 'em a bit, but he did make 'em laugh, and all he was trying to do was con 'em back to God—the ones who weren't too scared anyway, the ones who survived the spooking out. Stuie figured the devil could have the rest. "Exactly," says God (well the Authorities representing God). "That is precisely why your plan to kiss the devil will work; because you have scared a lot of people into the devil's domain. Well done." Stuie became a bit sullen. He'd never seen the other side of things, that he'd actually scared people into the devil's arms. "Oh, well, what the fuck," he exclaims. "Up one, back one."

Then God says, "Stuie you can't love the devil by denying him. You have to go out and be the devil and feel what that is like, and then you can love the devil through your knowledge of yourself. Try being the Prince of Darkness a bit and see what it teaches you." The Prince of Darkness was not Stuie's cup of tea, until he found out what incredible fun it can be. (Of course, all these conversations happened while Stuie was in the temple, kinda dead. He'd also gone blind at the time, so he could be forgiven for getting a little muddled.)

It turned out that the body Stuie inhabited was not really dead, just comatose. To cut a long story shorter, Stuie rose again the next day a very different person. He pondered for a while—he wasn't sure what he might do next as there were no instructions from God in his pocket as there had been in the past. So, our Stuie decided he'd try being the Prince of Darkness for a bit as it's heaps of fun and you can scare the fat controllers every time you go boo...especially if they have their shadow hidden deep inside. Anyway, it was the only way to get to the devil and getting there was all part of getting to the Lady of the Lake. Stuie had prayed to the Lady of the Lake more than anyone ever before him.

Being the Prince of Darkness was intoxicating beyond words, it was like trick or treat, except there were no treats just the tricks. Stuie spent a bit of time spooking out the righteous ones, trying to scare them back to God. Then, acting on the advice of a living saint, Stuie saw that light and dark were one and the same; and the saint reminded Stuie that if he got too good at being the Prince of Darkness he would wind up with the job full time. Stuie hated that idea. He liked the novelty, but the nine-to-five tick-tock rhythm of the Prince of Darkness filled Stuie with a terrible dread. Anyway, he knew that the devil only really wanted a bit of attention, so he'd call to him at night, trying to entice him with the offer of a free blowjob, but the devil hid away. (I think the devil figured out that Stuie didn't really mean the bit about a free blowjob.) Anyway, Stuie's instruction was to kiss the devil, there was no mention of blowjobs. Stuie can go over the top sometimes. He's not quite past the 'trying to please' bullshit he learned in childhood.

After a while, Stuie got pissed off with the devil's evasion, so he hired a few angels to help him out. He could have hired them years ago but he never thought to ask for help—another one of his faulty traits. The angels wandered about 'til they found the devil sulking in a bar, crying into his beer. The devil knew that once he accepted Stuie Wilde's love, his days of being a proper devil would be numbered, as a part of him would have to come over to the other side.

Stuie had a sense of responsibility and felt, rightly or wrongly, that he was the only one available to handle the devil—not only because he would take on just about anything but because he had passed the test as the Prince of Darkness, which meant he could relate to light and dark.

Finally, Stuie shows up on the angel's tip off, kisses the devil and says, "You're an okay dude but try to improve ya ways." Next, he gives the devil an unexpected whack in the mouth, and then he holds the devil for half an hour, telling him over and over that he loves him. Some of the devil's blood fell on Stuie's white shirt.

At first Stuie was annoyed by the stain, but then he saw it was a blessing and that it would come in very handy for frightening priests like the Irish Christian Brothers who sexually abuse young boys. If fact, it turns out that there is a whole encyclopedia on what you can do with the devil's blood, but Stuie didn't know that at the time. Anyway, he was about to be retired from the Prince of Darkness role, though he didn't know it until the Lady of the Lake showed up.

Here's the best bit. Stuie said to the devil, "Listen up brother, you're a bit of a fuckwit, but you have your uses. Why don't you work for me? I used to work for God trying to trick people back to the light, but there were many who were too scared, they couldn't stand the light. I'd make 'em walk on fire to see if they were any good but the majority were too up themselves or too righteous or too this or too that—scared mostly. Not many made it. Some went part of the way, but out of 100,000 or so, only about 1,500 made it to the river bank across from God. You must have fed off the stragglers, you devil you.

"If we can't trick 'em with kindness, let us trick 'em with fear, whaddayasay my little mate, devil that you are? Let me love you from time to time, after all, you and me are in the same business of getting folk back to God." The devil warmed up to Brother Stuie once he realized that he, the devil, had been working for God all along. He felt quite useful and proud. Anyway, he had to pretend to be polite as Stuie had him pinned down and the devil wasn't up for another whack in the mouth.

Stuie continues, "Let me give you the list of the ones I'm looking for—the missing members, so to speak." The devil was quite happy cos he now realized he was off Stuie's hook. He says, "You mean you will let me go around and scare this lot on your list?" And Stuie said, in the way he always does, "Cooorse ya can."

So Stuie gives the devil another drink, pops a list of names of about 100,000 people he wants back into the devil's shirt pocket, and says, "Don't be too long, and don't get distracted or I'll give ya another whack in the mouth." Stuie is quite a peaceful bloke, but if he gives you a whack it has velocity and fuckin' hurts—the devil knew that first hand as his mouth was still bleeding.

Then Stuie went back to Ireland and he invited the bloke he calls Tripitaka, the living saint, to stay with him a while. In a quiet moment he says, "I tried to save 100,000 but most were too unsure or too scared to see it. I felt it was urgent, that they should see how much danger they were in. Most got hung up on thinking they were special. The rest needed status, money, disastrous relationships, babies, blah, blah, anything to distract them from the path. I had to send the devil after them. I'm not sure if he can be relied on. It was a hell of a job even finding him. What do I do now?"

The saint said, "Rest for a bit Stuie and then learn French cos you'll need it, as there are about as many assholes in France as there are in your native England."

"I got a few real warriors out of England," said Stuie, "and they are good fighters, the English, as are the Scots, but the rest of the folk are a mess and too much in the mind to be of any service." "True," said the saint. "Let the devil have them."

"I also tried hard in Ireland," said Stuie, "but they are often a bit confused and that weakens them. They pretend that some of their Irish spirit died in the famine. Of course, it didn't die in the famine, but they like to crack a tale of woe. Many of the strong ones left anyway."

"True," said the saint, "but some of the strong ones are coming back, and anyway they are all good at drinking and poetry."

"Yes," said Stuie. "I love them for that. What else could one need?"

"By the way," said Stuie. "The love of my life is Irish, but I can't tell her I love her for if I do she will run away."

The saint said, "Stuie, you must stop hankering for what you cannot have."

"Okay," says Stuie, "but can we go out boozing and fighting just to release a bit of energy."

✦ ✦ ✦ ✦ ✦

Stuie and the saint are having a drink in a pub and Stuie is waiting for something strange to happen. He says to the saint, "You're a poof and a wimp. When the fight starts, head to the restroom or you might get hurt. I love you, but I don't want to have to explain to God how one of his saints got bashed up in a pub just because I can't have the girl I want."

The saint leaned forward and said, "Stuie, what is her name?" And Stuie whispered it and all one could hear over the clatter of the pub was that it began with an H.

Tripitaka said to Stuie, "You, brother, are full of bullshit. It's all in your mind. If you really wanted her you could have her, as she has got a thing about her dad, and you seem like her dad to her. Truth be known, Stuie, you don't actually want her and if she landed on ya thingy you'd soon get bored and you'd be off hankering for her best mate. Wake up t'ya self, man, wake up."

"Fuck it, let's fight," says Stuie slightly frustrated by all this romance bullshit. Just then a fellow from the Garda (Ireland's National Police Service) shows up and tries to arrest Stuie for being disorderly. Stuie says, "Excuse me, Sir, why don't you take off your uniform and let's fight like citizens."

The copper declines and offers to arrest Stuie. Stuie says, "You can't arrest me cos I haven't done anything yet, and anyway I'm the Princes of fucking Darkness and if you do arrest me I'll torment you and your family 'til the end of your days. I'll give you diseases you have never heard of and I may enjoy making your life a fucking misery."

The copper takes a bit of a fright cos he realizes something very odd is going on—and what's this 'lets fight like citizens' caper? Who the fuck is this little fellow who claims to be the Prince of Darkness? In the end, the police officer makes peace and offers to drive Stuie and the saint back to the presidential suite in the fancy hotel where they were staying.

While Stuie was in the back of the cop car, he silently blessed the copper with the kind of words the Pope might use, "Ecce crucem domini…blah, blah," (the officer was Catholic). And it wasn't long after that, was it, that the fellow got a promotion rather unexpectedly, so all's well that ends well.

Stuie is now sitting in the hotel room at one in the morning, rather bored, formulating his theory on fighting. The saint, his advisor, has gone to bed. Stuie reckons you can always win a fight, even against bigger blokes, by silently using your mind to persuade the fellow to let you whack him first. "It," says Stuie with an impish grin, "is a lot easier than you think." Most people are afraid to start a fight and only feel justified getting involved once the fight has begun. So all you do is look at the left side of their brain and silently say, "Would you mind if I take over the responsibility of starting this fight. I'll whack you and that will give you the righteous excuse to whack me back." Of course, Stuie doesn't mention that when he whacks you, you get hit 25 times in less than three seconds, and you usually can't whack him back as you are often lying on the floor helpless, snorting blood, looking up, admiring the chandelier in the lobby.

All these thoughts circled in Stuie's mind and, anyway, Stuie had seen Fight Club and he realized that fighting people that are bound to lose is violence, while fighting people who will kick the crap out of you is redemption. Stuie now feels better and decides to quit fighting forever. His mind then turns once more to romance. It's about 1:30am and the saint, his advisor, has gone to bed, so Stuie starts pondering what to do next. His deep inner soul says, "Let go of romance and do unconditional love instead. It works a whole lot better and it doesn't hurt like romance because you never wind up feeling that you belong to anyone, or that you own him or her. Now go back to the forest Stuie and meet the real thing, the Goddess. The Bodhisattva Kuan-Yin is willing to see you now."

Stuie wakes up from a dream about the Goddess and the Lady of the Lake. He grabs the saint and says, "We're off to Australia, get ya kicker back in ya hand bag. Airport." Stuie knew he'd find the Lady of the Lake there.

It might seem odd that you'd find a Celtic goddess in Australia, but when Stuie knows something to be true, he almost never makes a mistake—he's irritatingly fuckin' accurate. What can you do? Anyways, he had met his shadow, acquired the heat, kissed the devil, given up on romance and embraced unconditional love, and finally agreed to stop carousing and fighting. He was ready, though his silver bangles, silk clothes, and spices for his hair were still in storage. Never mind, they weren't needed.

The Lady didn't come the way Stuie expected. He thought he'd be directed to a lake in the Australian bush, but instead she came and found him. He was lying on his couch at four in the morning and suddenly there she was at his feet standing very still and watching him. She was nothing like the pre-Raphaelite women in the Camelot paintings. Though she was very beautiful. She reminded Stuie of a nature spirit, for though she had a feminine form she had cloven feet and some fur and feathers on her body. Her hair was very dark and her face very beautiful and serene, but her eyes were very scary. There was a white ring both around and in the center of the pupils—looked like a bull's eye to Stuie.

Stuie said, "Your eyes are very scary ma'am. I'm too old in the tooth for this scary bullshit. I met the devil once, you know, and fought the Greys, now show me your good side." Whereupon something very odd happened: her eyes changed to become the most wonderful opal colored lights. They were the most radiantly beautiful eyes Stuie had ever seen, and she was the most beautiful woman he had ever set eyes upon. Her grace, strength, and godliness extended infinitely, beyond comprehension.

A geometric pattern in her left eye reminded Stuie of the circuit board of a computer. With it, she could see the future. She had all knowing. Stuie said that he loved her and he had looked for her for over a decade on and off. He asked her her name. She said, "She-She-La-La."

Stuie was overwhelmed with gratitude. He didn't feel worthy. He started to cry. He realized that after all these years of searching for the Goddess she had been with him all the time. She had never let him down. There was never a moment when she wasn't with him. Through his triumphs and his darkest hours, she was always there. Argante was Arthur's Lady of the Lake; She-She-La-La was Stuie's Lady of the Lake. There are lots of ladies of the lake, as many as there are goddesses.

She-She-La-La then enters Stuie's body via the soles of his feet. He wasn't scared. He was ready. She extended herself through his body. When she got to his neck, she stopped and Stuie realized she could go no further as he was thinking too much. So he blanked his mind and she stretched into his head. But she was facing the wrong way. Stuie asked her to turn around and she did. She stayed like that for about an hour and Stuie experienced a type of celestial bliss. Then, she collapsed herself to about the size of a billiard ball and started to wander round Stuie's body. It tickled at times. She stayed in that form for three days. Stuie got the impression she was helping him to heal in some way.

Then she went very quiet. So Stuie decided to be silent for a day. She reappeared in the depths of that silence and showed Stuie things with her circuit-board eye. Stuie saw the fate of nations. He started to write it down but after a while he stopped, as he knew he would probably never be able to tell anyone what he had seen. After about 20 minutes, She-She-La-La turned the eye off and it all went quiet.

I begged Stuie to tell me what he had seen but he was very cagey. Though he did say a few things I found very odd. He said he didn't fancy real estate in Karachi or Tel Aviv. Neither the Arabs nor the Israelis would be allowed to keep Palestine; it would be taken from them and left fallow. Neither tribe is worthy. The Arabs because of their horrendous treatment and social imprisonment of women, and the Israelis because of their nastiness, expressed as military occupation and an elitist control trip. Look at their leaders. They're bigger Nazis than Goebbels or Hitler ever were. Dawn Trader country, I'd say. Stuie said that it was agreed about 50 years ago that the Jews would only have a short-term lease in Palestine. Their tenure of these lands is to show the world what the covert 'dark' really looks like. That is why the Arab-Israeli story is in the news every day, yet no one really gives a fuck for either group. It's to teach people. That is also why the The New York Times runs a Palestine story almost every day forever on its front page.

The Arabs play 'poor me' look at the rotten Israelis, and the Israelis play 'poor me' we deserve to victimize these people and dominate these lands that aren't ours cos we were victimized by the Nazis.

He went on to say, "Iceland will prosper." I asked why. He said, "Cows, Iceland is very clean and pure."

"Cows?" I asked. Stuie's reply was, "Fuckin' spooky." He said humans look like the Nazis to cows. The cows tried to fight back by giving people cancer. But they couldn't kill people fast enough to make up for the numbers of their own spirit-tribe that was being exterminated, so they asked for help. The Authorities suggested that the cows' best escape, for the moment anyway, was to pretend to die—they'd be given another chance elsewhere. And it was reluctantly agreed that they would be allowed to leave Mad Cow disease behind as a pay back. Mad Cow disease rots your brain. "Work it out," said Stuie. He concluded by saying that almost all domestic animals are a great danger to meat-eating humans, except pigs. Cos once the domestic animals saw the way out offered to the cows, they all voted for the final solution. Stuie concluded by saying, "Wasn't it a clever ploy that pigs, the only safe animal for human consumption, have been labeled by the Jews as 'unclean.' Never trust anyone, it's all backwards."

Stuie also said New Zealand would go bankrupt. The Maoris tried to capture the spirit of New Zealand by pretending they had been wronged by the white man. In fact, it was the Maoris who paddled over the water from other Pacific islands to slaughter the original inhabitants of New Zealand. The Maoris have no right to New Zealand whatsoever and they should paddle back home-—if anyone wants such an angry group of wastrels. Kiri Te Kanawa, the Maori opera singer, was sent by God to save the Maori soul, but she got so hung up with glitz, money, and pretending to be a white woman that her efforts were wasted. God's a bit pissed off about that. God also told Stuie in a quieter moment that the Maoris are angry cos they know that deep down no one really believes the Maori lie. There is no point in worrying about them; it's a waste of time. Anyway, many of the Maoris will die from a terrible incurable disease, which makes the blood go translucent. (The good one's will survive; there's good and bad in every tribe.) Stuie has seen it but he doesn't have enough medical knowledge to identify it. In the mirror of those diseased cells they will see the lie of what they are. The planet will soon be rid of many of the worst of the Maoris, which ought to cheer up the other New Zealander's a bit. Though Kiri Te Kanawa will not be there to sing at their requiem, which is a pity because she does have a nice voice. Stuie concluded by saying the Australian Aboriginals are safe for the moment, as they have a good heart deep within.

After She-She-La-La, Stuie was looking for something to do so he started to teach women in secret about the Goddess and her etheric ways. He showed them how to fashion their power and hone it. He also showed them that there was no need to delve into their shame and lack of self-worth, which often arose from peer pressure and abuse, as there was a quicker way. Stuie realized it was She-She-La-La teaching the women, as half the teachings taught he never would have thought of in a million years. He only taught a few women as most of the women he knew would go potty at the idea of a male teaching them about femininity. But the women he taught went out with the knowledge. Stuie said that after She-She-La-La showed him what he needed to know, he realized that he was right about femininity lying at the mathematical center of the universe, and that modern women knew little or nothing about femininity beyond what might be found in a magazine at the newsagents. Stuie says that femininity has very little to do with sex. Though most women don't know that and use sex to buy themselves male protectors in a scary world. He feels it's sad that women suffer so much emotional and psychological pain for no reason at all. It's part of the control trip to make them feel they are less than they are. Stuie says all women are worthy. He wondered what to do about it. He said you can't just put it in a book, cos a woman's mind might accept the concept intellectually, but her feelings are often too shame ridden—and that will always overrule the mind. Anyway, any concept of the mind is never the real thing. Women have to go and see the Goddess to get it. Then and only then will they know for certain that all women are worthy. But because they have to go through a mini-death to get to her, it limits the numbers that make the journey.

6

Misinformation and the False Gods

I'm back! I thought it best to leave for a bit, as I get embarrassed about stories that feature me. The story of my search for the devil, the celestial heat, and the Lady of the Lake is a true one. Though my encounter with the devil is, of course, allegorical. Yet in a strange way it wasn't far from the real truth—the attack by the clawed entity really happened in October 1999, and a year later my crown chakra was still not quite mended. Better now though.

WHERE ARE WE?

Obviously our body is on Earth but our consciousness, what we really are, is everywhere. Even our body is everywhere in a strange way. We are in a solid and yet not-solid reality and that reality is in a hologram. If you look at a hologram and see that it has an image of a horse in it, everywhere you look the complete image will appear. You may make the error of saying there are 100 horses in the hologram, but in fact there is only the one horse repeated 100 hundred times. In this reality, there is only one of you but you are repeated everywhere. I've seen a mirror reality of another version of me—it looked the same. I was lying down and the 'other me' was joined to the 'real me' at my feet. It was lying down also, stretched away from me. I don't understand it well enough to explain. It could well have been just another hologram version.

You are also at the center of the universe; so am I, and so is Aunt Maud in Ohio. If you and I are sitting having a coffee at a table across from each other, it's hard to see how both of us can be at the center of everything, as one of us ought to be slightly off center. But it's not so. You are in your hologram at the center of your universe and I am in mine, and we are both in each others'. Every part of the universe (and maybe other universes and other dimensions) is everywhere. The mystical idea that we are all connected is correct.

You are everything. Everything emits a feeling. So you are all the feelings of the universe. Therefore, if you want to know what is round the next corner you only have to blank your mind and enter the feeling. Remember, subtle feeling is ESP not emotion. Of course, most people are not used to listening to their subtle feelings for information, as they are either all mental activity, or they confuse feelings with emotions.

What seems to be an extra sensory perception of feelings is, in fact, your primary perception. The mind and its free will are the override. They enter a guessing game when in fact you already have all the answers, you always did have. You also know exactly what is going on and what is about to happen next. All human action rises from a hidden subconscious impulse and that impulse has a feeling. When you get good at it, you can 'feel' the very subtle impulses that will occur in the future. After you master listening to your feelings, you don't have to plan or think. It's all obvious, minute-by-minute. It's such a relief. Of course, once your life becomes immediate, you won't be able to plan very far ahead, as at any moment your subtle feelings might cancel your mental plan; however, it does allow you to be right all the time. Your subtle feelings are never wrong.

Once you follow the subtle plan, life becomes magical—but you will not at first understand the synchronicity of life that is all around you, weaving its magic. Yes, the universe is close-by and all around you. Simple. That is why I say get rid of free will; it's a disaster and part of the control trip. You're probably a slave to it. Drop it. Stop searching and planning, stop it. Stop pretending your intellect knows what to do. Feel out what you ought to do next. You'll get good at it very quickly. At first you may make a few mistakes by letting emotion or thinking get in the way, but you will soon master it.

Soon nothing will be able to hide from you, and after a while your subtle feelings will talk to you in more complex ways, like visions. If everyone went with their feelings, this zoo, this prison, would fall apart. We'd leave the world of emotion and mind and enter the Kingdom of Heaven, as our subtle feelings are part of the Kingdom of Heaven. They offer us the real truth.

Imagine a world where there was only real truth. Where your stockbroker had to tell the truth, where lawyers were not allowed to lie, where everyone had to admit their true intentions. At first, it would be mayhem, but once everyone had been caught out lying a few times; they'd soon follow the game plan and would have to quit lying or be ostracized.

The lies of the world are all pervasive. They are everywhere. In every corner you look. People pretend to be righteous and honest; people pretend they have your interests at heart while screwing you at every moment of the day. People say they love you, but if they do from emotion or mind, they are lying. Love that comes from the mind is usually just a social nicety, like saying, "Good morning." If you listen carefully you will hear when someone's love comes from their mind, not from their feelings; you will notice the hollow clang in their voice. A mental "I love you" has a tinny feel to it. Love that comes from emotion is usually not worth having either as it's laced with a need that screams, "I love you, but love me back. I'm insecure—don't leave me." Only unconditional love from your subtle feelings is right.

Where are you? You are at the center of a subtle feeling. Let go of free will, it's a nightmare and inaccurate—use subtle feelings instead, they are never wrong. Stop guessing what the outcome will be, stand inside the feeling of the outcome and you will know.

Where are Heaven and Hell?

You guessed it. They are right here, inside you, inside me, inside every molecule of reality. Both are in the hologram, your hologram and mine. God is both heaven and hell and the devil is the same—they are all in the same hologram. If you can love the devil and the dark side, and not be scared of it, you are free. That does not mean you should embrace evil, it just means you should have looked at the evil within you, forgiven yourself, and improved your ways. And you should embrace the evil of others and love them for their weakness and dysfunction.

75

There is no real good and evil, everything is one. You choose the quality of what you want to see, well your emotions and attitude do.

So what is hell? Hell is an emotion. It's where most of the fat controllers of this world will end up. The insidious nature of their inhuman behavior will take them to a fat controller's world, except there they will find that they are the ones being controlled. When you hold a person tightly by the wrist, you imagine that you control them, and if they don't know what they are doing, you do. But if you hold a martial arts expert by the wrist, he'll soon be walking you about, towing you along by your grip of him. His ability to make a move on you is subject to how hard you are holding on to him—your imagined control of him. The harder you hold him, the more lethal he will become, as he will use your grip of him to break your arm and will put you in a disadvantaged position where anything might happen.

Hell is holding on. Heaven is letting go; love is letting go. Letting go can be scary. The mind is not usually up to letting go. But that is the nature of control. It seeks ultimate power. All power is a control trip. But all control controls the controller. You might be the president of a large company where your ego can flourish in its illusion of its importance. In fact, you don't have a life. The company, its employees, and your customers control you. You are in a comfy prison if the corporation is making money and in an appalling prison if it is losing money. Both are prison camps. When your spirit finds itself in a prison it will seek a way out. It will figure out a way to bankrupt the company, or it will create an incident or a disease, anything to escape. Your corporation will be faced with endless problems, especially if the company has been going for a long time. Businesses usually only work while they are new and creative, but once the humdrum sets in, the company's cast of characters, the staff, the owners, and so on, usually find a way to kill it off or change it.

Control is demonic. Trying to control another person is hell—their hell, your hell. Almost all domestic violence is control related. He whacks her cos he's frustrated at the control she is trying to exercise over him, or because she won't be subjected to his Nazi control trip. Or, she whacks him for the same reasons—two Nazi controllers fighting turf wars over who will run the prison.

What is jealousy? It's the mind's reaction to a loss of control, or the imagined loss of control. If you don't have to control, you can't be jealous, can you? Jealousy is a fascist emotion. In the realm of subtle feeling you will love your partner unconditionally. You won't try to own them and they won't try owning you. You will assist them to whatever is best for them in this life, even if that means they move out. Divorce is the result of unresolved control trips. Each hires a good liar and they enter a court that pretends to be interested and the control trip eventually gets sorted out.

What is romance? It's a drug trip. When you find someone who pleases you, endorphins are released into your bloodstream. You become slightly intoxicated or, in severe cases, demented. The same happens to your chosen partner if they are in love with you. After a few months, the novelty wears off and you either part or you try to sustain the drug high by entering into a formal or informal marriage contract. What is marriage? It's a control trip. It's a contract formalizing the flow and supply of drugs—brain drugs. Why does infidelity usually cause pain? Because of the loss of control and the loss of an imagined immortality. It feels like a death to the one who is at the wrong end of the infidelity. It usually angers them. They see it as life threatening. It also usually triggers abandonment issues (fear). If you love someone unconditionally, there is no more faithful or unfaithful. If they go off with someone else, let them go. Just insist they keep you properly informed so you can make your decisions based on truth not lies.

Sex is both one of our greatest pleasures and greatest tormentors. Sex can hurt. It often requires you to let go and be intimate. It hurts the female if the male satisfies himself then leaves without caring for her emotions. It hurts the male if she suddenly says "no," triggering rejection. It can also hurt him if he is not very good at having sex—shame kicks in. Sex is a business in our modern world. It's the glue that holds together most romances and marriage contracts. As glue, it becomes another part of the financial or emotional bargain, which requires you to sell your soul down the river.

When you can join with your partner and see them as eternal, and when you can let go and not be a victim of it all, or be victimized by your need for it, then it becomes a wonderful thing. When sex is used to patch up a gaping hole in your relationship, it's futile. Sex is one way you learn to love yourself. It's how you come to see yourself as worthy and beautiful. Most men know nothing about sex and don't know how to control ejaculation. Women will always have the advantage in that department. Most men know nothing about women and they don't know how to talk to a woman in her language. It can make the world a lonely place for lots of women. In turn, women should stop trying to use men as security, trying to fill a gap within themselves. No man can fill the gap in a woman; he's not some sort of psychological plasterer. Instead, she should fill her own gap and attempt to enter her goddess energy, and only come back to her partner, male or female, once she has sorted that out. If she doesn't do that, sex may cause bitterness, anger, shame, guilt, resentment, and confusion. She may deny her need altogether. Only sex under the rules of unconditional love makes any sense long-term. Most other sex is part of a subtle business arrangement or control trip.

We attempt to exercise control to create the illusion of immortality—it also grants us a phony security. In controlling others, we stand over them. So we are psychologically distant from them, above them. We psychologically distance ourselves from other people to make ourselves important and to avoid their fate. The fate of death. Control seeks to avoid that fate. We hope to become more secure, but we are in fact less secure as we are less spontaneous and less fluid.

CONTROL, BY ITS VERY NATURE,
ALWAYS CONTROLS THE CONTROLLER
AS WELL AS THOSE
BEING CONTROLLED.

THE FALSE GODS OF IMMORTALITY

One of the biggest lies in the world is the false gods of immortality. That is not to say you are not eternal, it's only to say that our human body will die. Importance places itself above others, seeking immortality by distancing itself from the common man. Glamour is the same. Glamour seeks observers. As I've said in my other books at length, in seeking observers the ego seeks to make itself more solid, thus more alive and less dead. An atomic particle becomes solid only once it is observed; before someone observes it, it exists in a hazy wave state, everywhere and nowhere at the same time. Glamour is a false god of immortality. Vanity is too.

There are hundreds of false gods: arrogance, the class system, and snobbery to name a few common ones. The concept of royalty, the Chosen One, the god-like being who has power over common people, as an accident of birth or by the sword, is a false god. No one is above you and you should not be above or below others. 'God save our gracious Queen' is a prayer to the false god of her hoped for immortality. Royalty via birth will disappear. Despots will remain for a while, 'til the Dawn Trader shows up anyway.

When materialism seeks to gratify a need, it is not a false god of immorality just gratification; but when it seeks observers, with say the flashy sports car, it is a false god. Arrogance is another way the ego deifies itself as a false god. Humility is the God.

To adopt a healthy lifestyle may be your pleasure and choice. Yet if you adopt a practice to sustain immortality, it becomes a false god. If you jog because you like banging your knees to a pulp, then do so. If you jog because you want to live forever, tut, tut. It killed Jim Fix the jogging guru. Clue? Do you imagine you can prolong your life by even ten seconds? Do you know about the nature of time? On the masculine timeline you have free will and you can change anything, or so you would like to imagine. But there are two other timelines. One is eternal and one is feminine. On the feminine timeline you can't change anything for it runs backwards in time. So everything has already happened. Do you really think you are traveling from birth to death? Welcome to the mirror world. Welcome to a phony immortality.

If being a vegetarian gives you energy, or you love animals so much you don't care to eat them, adopt it. If you are a vegetarian because it makes you feel holy and special, dump it quick. A little known fact is that lettuce is very toxic, as is cabbage—especially raw lettuce and raw cabbage. Lettuce is the Dawn Trader appearing as an almost tasteless green leaf. Stay away from lettuce unless you fancy it cooked.

What of spiritual practices? The spiritual practice of sitting in quiet contemplation telling God from your heart that you adore it, and that you are so very grateful for being here on Earth, is not a false god. It doesn't seek immortality, specialness, or status of any kind.

Spiritual practices that seek status will trap you and often make you ill, worse than that they trap you in what we erroneously call the afterlife. Here you will end up in the company of a lot of other immortality seekers, drifting around not comprehending where you all are or what you are doing. A church that celebrates life, instructs people, and allows them to leave unhindered is not a false god. Anything that stands between you and God is a false god. As soon as anyone promises to give you immortality, they become a false god. No one can promise you immortality and no one can grant you immortality as you are already immortal, no matter what you do in this life. Anyone who sells immortality via spiritual practices is an agent of the Sphere—no exceptions. Churches pretend they will take you to God. But decades pass and many fail to notice that the church has not delivered on its promise. Now, if someone tells you they will take you to God and they deliver you there and you see God and are in the presence of God, fair go.

What of the cult of the guru, the holy one, the ascended master? Tee hee! Anyone who sets him or herself up as holy or special has fallen face down into the Sphere—splat! Are there any exceptions? None. If they then use their feigned holiness to trap you for reasons of status, money, or power, it's totally demonic. All holy men are demonic except the few who don't realize they are holy. What you should be looking for is a descended master, one who knows he or she is nothing. One who is truly selfless, not just pretending to be selfless. One who loves you enough to take you back to nothing. I have a friend who is like a saint, but he doesn't know he is a saint and if you told him he is a saint, he'd walk away telling you not to be so silly.

What of spiritual teachers? A teacher who teaches you accurate stuff then disappears as soon as he or she is finished is probably not a false god. If they promise you a special status via membership of their organization, or if they trap you, manipulating you through fear from one course to another, then they become a false god. If they try to disallow you easy departure, then by the very nature of their control trip, they must be demonic. They must have a hidden agenda of money or power.

What of those who offer immortality? Rebirthers, yoga practitioners, and the like? Yoga will kill you if you do too much of it—never worked for the Indians either. Look at them if you dare to. Have you ever met anyone who did yoga regularly that wasn't weak and troubled and dying of pain in front of your eyes?

What of tantra? If you enjoy bonking or other people's company, then tantra is just organized enthusiastic bonking, which probably can't be bad. There a lot of Indians, so perhaps it works to help procreation. But if tantra is part of your immortality plan, try celibacy; it will work better for you.

What of those organizations that tell you you should meditate for hours every day? Serious bullshit merchants. What better way of controlling people? Forcing them to sit on the floor promising God and nirvana. Can they deliver God and nirvana? Or are they just pretending? When you don't get to nirvana, you're told to sit some more. You're told sitting is holy and special and that not sitting is less than holy. You're made to wear silly clothes—it will appeal to your sense of belonging and grants you a phony specialness. If you like to meditate, as I do, then do so for a short while not in the company of others, not as part of a special group, and not in silly clothes. If the practice makes you feel holy and special, discontinue it immediately until you return to your right mind.

What of clubs, elitist organizations, fancy country clubs, and so on? If you like the club no worries, if you like the elitism, piss on the gate and leave. The same applies to fancy hotels. If they give you genuine pleasure no problem; if you go to be observed, tut, tut.

What of regulation? Regulation that establishes order by consensus is administration. So we agree, for example, to stop at the red light and go at the green, and it becomes an administration of the flow of traffic, helping road users, by consensus, to proceed in a safe and orderly manner. Regulations that are imposed without consensus are control trips. They often have a hidden agenda, favoring some and disenfranchising or feeding off others. Regulation is your representative's way of saying he doesn't love you, while pretending that he represents and cares for you. Has a politician ever come to power and dissolved the very system that granted him or her specialness, status, and power? Do they ever cancel laws? Yes they do, only to replace them with other laws. No tax has ever been repealed. They have only ever been renamed. The hated Poll tax in the UK reemerged as Council tax. Ding! Ding!

What of the police force and the military? Where the police enforce consensus regulation, they become a part of the administration, upholding the desire for order, so to speak. That helps society. Where they enforce the will of the political elite, they become a part of the crime—welcome to the Gestapo. When the military defends a nation because it has been asked to, that is a great sacrifice and kindness. Attacking or establishing control over another nation is demonic.

Where is God?

God is not up, nor down, nor on an altar. God is everywhere. Is God outside you? No, it is not. You are God, well a part of it. So you might as well pray to yourself. "Our me, who art in heaven, hallowed be my name." Or, you can go with their inaccurate version. "Our father..." (God is not male), "...who art in heaven," (geographically not correct. God is not in heaven; It's everywhere, as you are). "...hallowed be thy name" (specialness). "Thy kingdom come..." (the

word 'come' says it is not already here—inaccurate).
"...thy will be done" (control, control). "...on Earth as
it is in heaven," implying Earth and heaven are separate,
thus establishing the right to lead people to heaven.
Follow my rules, my control, and you'll get to heaven,
which is some place else and not easy to get to. "Give us
this day our daily bread..." (Excuse me! God the baker?)
What's this rubbish? Yeast is a control trip; it feeds off
you while you think you are feeding off it. Who needs a
daily dose of yeast from God?

So never mind the toast, what about "and forgive
us our trespasses..." God can't forgive your trespasses.
It's not allowed to. Remember It can't go after the dark.
It is the dark. God is your trespass and everyone else's
sins as well. The only person who can forgive you your
trespasses is— _____ ?
(Please fill in the obvious.)

The only bit of the Lord's Prayer that is not wildly
inaccurate and designed to mislead or trap you is the bit
the Anglicans tacked on to the end. "For thine is the
kingdom..." (okay, creation is the kingdom let us say),
"...the power," (God does not wield power but as it is
everything we could say it is powerful. Though if you
asked God, "Are you powerful," it would grin and not
answer.), "Forever and ever, Amen." The 'forever and
ever' bit seems right, though no one has gotten to 'forever'
to find out for certain if God is still there. Maybe God

jumps ship just before the end and winds up some place else, beyond forever. I'm not sure what amen actually means or where it comes from. It must be a foreign word for I've had enough of listening to this bullshit, let's go on to something else.

7

Making
a Run for
Freedom

First, there is no run for freedom until you see the Sphere for what it is. Comprehending it all at once is a daunting task. All the popular information you receive is a lie, or it is sold to you backwards. The rest is couched in reasonableness (don't rock the boat) or it's offered with platitudes—ahh, but what about this and what about that?

It's all part of the barbed wire. We like restriction. It helps us to feel in control of our lives. It's vital for the mind to feel it is in charge—poor thing. Freedom is the wide-open space of 'anything can happen.' Most don't like lives where anything can happen. They want to be sure where they will be and what they will be doing months from now.

The first time I experienced true freedom I was terrified. I was about 30 years old, and one day I found myself in trance, hovering in all eternity with nothing under me to hold me up, just an eternal depth below. I got over it.

Ponder how you will make your run for freedom. We'll talk some more about the end run later but right now I doubt you could hack it, except in the most superficial, intellectual way. You can't really get it with your mind, remember that. The exit is perpetually hidden from your mind. It's deliberately obscured and hidden. Ding!

First, I ought to tell you what stands in your way, as a seemingly superior force stands at the gates of the prison. Never mind the human guards of social mores, regulations, and obligations, the camp commandant, or your free will—beyond all that is something seriously spooky. Wanna come look? As Cypher says in The Matrix, "It means buckle your seat belt Dorothy, Kansas is going bye-bye."

CHAPTER 7 TO BE CONTINUED...

8

FIELDS UPON FIELDS—
THE MECHANISM
OF CONTROL

The first part of this book might have seemed a bit brutal and direct, but you have to forgive me. Congratulations for getting through without reacting too much. I was only trying to get rid of those who didn't need to know this stuff. Most copies of this book are probably in the trash now, or are being mailed to people the 'spooked out' readers don't like: "Read this, it should stuff your life up real good," the note in the letterbox reads. Tee hee! Most people are best suited to resting comfortably in what they know and believing what they care to believe. Each has his or her own potential and

I have never insisted anyone go one way or another. All I have ever done is talk about what I know about the etheric world, or what I have discovered on my journeys to transdimensional worlds; I have never made what I know exclusive, secret, or hard to find. No one had to sit at the gate of the temple for ten years. Anyone who was willing was allowed to show up and review the buffet. Each chose as little or as much as they fancied.

Below I present the concepts introduced earlier on in the book in more detail, setting them out within a framework. I've repeated myself here and there to show you how an idea sits in the overall framework of control. So please forgive me if you find an idea has been restated. If you look at the idea left and right, up and down, you will see how it all clicks, like a jigsaw. Then, from time to time, put down the book and still your mind and be silent, and as long as you are not scared anymore, then the plan will talk to you. What is says is glorious. But it will always require you to let go. You can't take your mind, your life's story, your identity with you. (Sorry, sorry, love me, love me.)

✦ ✦ ✦ ✦ ✦

If you think this life has anything to do with you, you are lost in self-importance and ego and concepts you have been spoon-fed to trap you. You may not as yet understand that this life has nothing to do with you, but you may have had an inkling of it over the years— spirit may have talked to you in quiet moments. The part of the mind that thinks it is running your life is laboring under a delusion. Yes, mind pretends to run your life but that's all part of the con. It controls nothing even though it will insist the opposite. Your life has nothing to do with you or your mind (even if you think it does). It is part of something much bigger and more glorious. Once you can give yourself away, you'll see it.

The story of Stuie and the devil was part of the story of my process of giving myself away. The resurrection is more splendid than you can ever imagine. Once you no longer need to be you, which may take a while, and once you can give yourself away, then you become everything. Even a short glimpse of being everything will exhilarate you beyond words. If you are bored being 'you' then you are ready. Then again, maybe you need to be you for a bit longer, who knows? You do.

When I went on my search for the Lady of the Lake, I was totally pissed off with Stuie Wilde's antics, amusing as some of them were. I loved him for his bullshit, I cared for his soul, and I saw some worth in him—he was valid. But I also saw that there was no further for him to go without going over and over the same old stuff. I also saw that Stuie was ready to jump, as I'd witnessed the little lad in some very dodgy situations, staring down some

very scary stuff and refusing to give ground. "Well done,"
I says. Stuie laughs and says, "Lucky fluke." Then one
day I said, "Go to silence, Brother." He did and She-She-
La-La came for him. He was ready even though he
thought he wasn't. His mind was still holding on. Maybe
your version of She-She-La-La is waiting to show up in
your life. Go with her when she comes. She knows the
future, your future, our future.

THE REAL BOOK STARTS HERE

Laws are passed that control and legislate over every
minute of human activity—hundreds of thousands of
laws, an ever-increasing number of them created for
absolute control. Who writes these laws? Why does
anyone think they are necessary? Nothing ever seems to
be going in the right direction. The stranglehold over
people is closing in like an ever-tightening vice that turns
with every tick of the clock. As I said, no government ever
repeals any laws. We all know there is something wrong.
We see social injustice and we wonder why the system is
not fair. We can't figure out what exactly it is that doesn't
slot together, though we know there is something that's
not quite right. Morpheus in The Matrix refers to our
silent disquiet as "a splinter in your mind."

In the field theory that I lay out here, you will see
that we are being fed upon from above and on the

ground. I will identify what this hidden malaise really is and how you might design your life to escape it.

First, the tax burden is blatantly unfair. It mercilessly milks working people, forcing them into unnecessary activity. Of course, tax is voluntary. You could become a perpetual traveler and never live anywhere and then you legally don't owe tax. The rest are doomed to their chain gang life and its activity. I'll explain how activity is a control trip in a minute. Bureaucracy and regulations are piled ever higher, so that now a significant part of our spare time is taken up with unnecessary administration and compliance. The cost of that in time and money—accountant's fees, specialist advice, clerical expenses, postage and so on—is not reimbursed. It all stands as an extra hidden tax upon the purse of the individual. How has this come about? How is this situation sustained against the wishes of the electorate? Who in theory ought to be able to insist on legislation that would rectify the problem? Who are the people behind the scenes who continually work to disempower their fellow citizens? What is their agenda? Why are they doing it?

Below is a discussion on how the development and mechanism of control has come about, and within this somewhat bizarre and strange explanation, I will describe the other world experiences that in part brought me to these strange field theory conclusions. Like any theory, it is not complete, it stands to be modified, but it's more or less complete in today's terms. As we go through it you will see how it 'clicks' like one perfectly crafted cog being slotted into another. I found it strange, almost spooky at times. It took me a long while to accept it. But as I was led to these conclusions, I searched for a reasonable and logical exit—a more palatable theory, but I could find none. So the theory offers itself for consideration, controversial as it might be for some to accept. (By the way, I got the etheric part of this idea bit by bit from another place, not from anyone in this realm.)

In the 15th and 16th centuries, occult writings spoke of fields, invisible spheres of influence that surround Earth and humanity (the Sphere). A painting from around that time shows an initiate leaving the earth plane for the other worlds. In the painting, there are zigzag lines that we associate today with brainwaves and electricity. How they knew is a mystery. The great Austrian metaphysician, Rudolph Steiner, who dominated the scene in the 1920s and '30s, also spoke of the influence of the Sphere that surrounds humanity. He spoke of the Sphere before electromagnetic fields were properly understood, and certainly before quantum theory was properly worked out.

In my mid 30s and early 40s, I began, after a number of years of meditation and trance induction exercises, to see what was previously called the human aura and is now usually referred to as the subtle body or the etheric. Watching the etheric flash and move so vibrantly around a person with such great velocity got me used to the idea of the existence of subtle fields. I came to discover that all human thought, emotions and feelings, our entire evolution is inside the etheric. Real feelings are etheric, and not in the binary signals of the body's sensation.

Back to The Matrix for a moment. In it, Morpheus talks about fields-upon-fields, which he says exercise absolute control over humanity by placing us in a 'constructed reality' of the field's (the Sphere's) own making. Humans are oblivious to the horrifying reality that a superior force is controlling their lives. They are not aware that they sustain a computer-generated simulation, which appears to them as daily life. What I found so fascinating was that our reality, while not computer generated, is in effect very similar. We are in an electronic prison, an electromagnetic field that is being controlled by a devilish authority. In The Matrix, the computer-generated reality is sustained by unnamed AI (artificial intelligence) controllers with super human powers. These fields and life on Earth are designed to support the needs of the superior beings. In the film, humans are grown for their body heat as BTUs (British Thermal Units). It's the heat and vitality of humans that sustains the fields and provides power to the AI controllers. Humans are grown as a crop to sustain the field without humankind ever suspecting the truth.

In September 2000, I met a very knowledgeable scientist who also talked about the fields upon fields. He said that they have come about as a result of humanity's emotions and thought forms over the ages; but the fields also have their own identity, their own evolution. He said the fields feed off humanity for sustenance. By feeding off humanity the fields attempt to sustain a false immortality. He said the fields' intrinsic nature is one of control. Just as a magnet controls iron filings, arranging them in orderly patterns.

The fields have become stronger and stronger as the world's population has increased dramatically since World War II and as people's energy has risen and activity increased. As we have become more aware, more individual, and more mobile, so the strength of the controlling fields has grown. Inside the fields are entities that have evolved within it. Whether these entities are birthed inside the field or whether they are transdimensionals from another dimension who are attracted to the field for sustenance, we don't know as yet. Of course, the idea of an entity being birthed inside a field is not foreign to us. Our human body is in an electromagnetic field, as is the whole earth plane, and we are birthed here. The idea that there might be other fields and other entities, while 'way out' to some people, is fairly obvious to others. Microbes, for example, are an evolution invisible to the human eye that remained hidden for tens of thousands of years until we invented microscopes powerful enough to see them. They are a hidden evolution. Remember this; the cells of your body are only about 10 percent human, the other 90 percent is all the microbes that live on and in your body, considering it to be their home planet as we consider Earth to be our home. Just as a microbe isn't human, the entities that live inside the Earth's etheric don't have to be human either, they just have to exist there and exhibit intelligent behavior.

Jose Escamilla, the Hispanic-American researcher, has photographed an etheric being, an evolution that he calls Flying Rods. These rods are a few inches to several feet long. They have fins that oscillate along etheric bodies. The rods fly through the air at high speed and they also exist underwater. They have probably always been here. They are another evolution that has remained unseen until recently with the advent of the video camera that can now record at a speed of 30 frames a second. The human eye can't differentiate details at 1/30th of a second but a camera can. Escamilla discovered the flying rods by accident when his video camera was left on one day. While editing his film, he noticed the strange flying rods zip into the frame, turn, and then fly out again, all in the space of a few frames. He has since filmed hundreds of the flying rods. In a clip I saw, there are two people talking when a rod flies into shot at about waist height; it moves round them and then flies out of shot again. What are flying rods? No one knows, least of all Escamilla. But they are part of the fields upon fields.

They are birthed in some way and evolve and grow. They definitely exhibit intelligence, as their motion through the air is not haphazard. They maneuver intelligently, making turns, attempting to avoid solid objects, and so on. When they accidentally hit something solid, they disappear in a faint flash of light, like a mini-explosion.

Humans are not so much a physical evolution (our body is just a sensory gathering mechanism), we are an etheric evolution. We don't know as yet if there are any other human-like evolutions in our galaxy or even in the universe. But we do know there are other etheric evolutions. I'll now talk about these and my experiences with them, and how I feel they are linked to the fields of control.

By its very nature, the desire for control is a desire for immortality. As I said in my book Whispering Winds of Change, control is addictive to the ego. When one seeks to dominate, what one is really seeking is a god-like power over others. So a Third World despot who executes some and elevates others sets himself up as a god over his people. To be god-like grants the ego the illusion that it is different from and separate to the destiny of man, which of course is to die. All those who seek to control and dominate, do so as a death-avoidance mechanism. The death they hope to avoid may not be a literal death but simply the death of an idea: the status quo, a job, or a special importance or privilege a person may enjoy. It's the death of their cherished ideas, as well as the death of the body, that they try to avoid.

Immortality, of course, is a false god of the ego, which seeks to remain ever young, potent and powerful. It squirms to avoid the physical plane's Second Law of Thermodynamics, which requires everything in the universe to degenerate and cool down—a heat death, which is measured at -273°C (absolute zero). Eternity is warm and that is a factor of spirit not a factor of the physical plane. In its most basic form, the warmth of eternity forms part of our nostalgia for God—the desire for spirit to return to eternity, our true god-like nature, which gives us heat. Our world is cold compared to the world of spirit. Our people are cold, spookily cold. I have often wondered how we are supposed to save them. In theory, a strong person could redeem them, but in practice it's unlikely. It makes me sad. Many fell so low they could not escape. There was no one that cared for them enough; but in a way it was their fault. They had such little goodness in them, no real goodness, just a phony social demeanor. Mr. Nice Guy, yeah, yeah— kick the little dog in the head when no one's lookin'.

It's not surprising that people have headed off the path, as our little planet is littered with false prophets and false gods of desire, like the ego's desire for immortality. Look at how Americans worship at the altar of longevity, cosmetic surgery, facelifts, jogging (which kills you anyway), this fad, and that diet. Then there's the modern American obsession with rigorously controlling everyone's habits: no smoking, no drinking, no sex, no drugs, no jay walking, no this, and no that. Here's your condom, stick it over your brain in case you get impregnated with any non-authorized ideas. Americans are so strange; they keep laboring under the illusion that they are important, that somehow the world couldn't manage without them. It makes me giggle sometimes. It's hopelessly pathetic to think you are important. It is even more hopeless to say so. Like the bimbo in the hair commercial who tosses her locks about, "Look at me, look at me, I am so lovely." The commercial ends with her saying "because I am worth it." Cringe, cringe—poor girl. Stay away from the shampoo in case it seeps through your skull into your brain and makes you as egocentric and as mindless as her. Remember, if you think this journey has anything to do with you, then you have completely lost the plot.

Metaphysician, writer and spiritual teacher, Rudolph Steiner, who was very prominent in the 1920s, identified six dark forces in the world, three he called

Luciferian forces and three, Ahrimanic forces. Ahriman is the Zoroastrian word for the negative or dark force. Steiner said that Ahrimanic forces were corporal forces of control that exercise power day to day, on the ground, so to speak. The forces of Lucifer were those that sought to control man's spirituality and his relationship to God.

The forces of Ahriman were identified as the media, which seeks to control and police ideas, which in effect silences the alternative voice of humankind. The second Ahrimanic force is the printing and control of money, and the creation of debt, which enslaves the nation state, and so enslaves workers who pay unnecessary taxes to cover the interest on phony paper money that was never real, just newly printed. Paper that was worthless yesterday is today placed upon citizens as an encumbrance—a phony debt upon which interest has to be paid to those pretending to manage the economy on the people's behalf. This phony debt forces workers into additional, unnecessary activity in order to pay the interest due. It traps them and feeds the fields. A third Ahrimanic force is the manufacture and sale of arms. That is, the selling of fear to enrich the manufacturers. It enslaves the populace with fear and the financial burden of paying for those arms. The terrible irony is, arms kill ordinary working people—those who are falsely burdened with the cost of them. Bombs, rockets, and bullets rarely kill those who commission the manufacture of them.

Since Steiner's time we have seen another force of darkness that is a sub-set of the information control via the media—it is the gathering and control of information by computers. With the advent of computers and the electronic era, all citizens are under perpetual scrutiny and surveillance. Those who like to watch us thrill at the idea of being able to keep us under observation, and they spend whatever it takes to enable those systems.

Any institution that seeks to unnecessarily control citizens is by its very nature an extension of the fields and an Ahrimanic force. Its action may be legal under a country's law but it is illegal under God's law. Not that God has a law, just to say that certain actions liberate, others imprison.

Steiner identified the Luciferian forces as those that seek to cripple or control human spirituality. Any institution or individual that sets itself or himself up as an intermediary between you and God is by its very nature a Luciferian or devilish force. The cult guru that sells himself as the special emissary of God, or a church, like the Catholic Church, that places itself between its parishioners and God, is in effect a controlling influence. In the case of the Catholic Church, it uses the fear of damnation and retribution as the cattle prod of its control. In fact, any religion that does not vouchsafe human individuality and set them free, is by its nature a part of the control fields. Strangely, the Tibetans and the dark nature of their teachings about the dead and the Bardo, and Buddhism's obsession with the negation of self (which is anti-spiritual) falls into the definition of a Luciferian force. It is interesting that Hitler was obsessed with the Tibetans. He sent regular Nazi delegations off to Tibet to make contact and carry back the Tibetan teachings. Hitler's spirituality and Tibet therefore have something in common. I know Tibet is flavor of the month right now, but that is propaganda; there is something very dark about Tibet that is not obvious at first glance.

Spiritual elitism, the cult of the Chosen Ones (the cult of the divine personality), the ascended master, the spiritual leader who stands between you and God, and anyone who sets himself or herself up as a god-like entity, falls into the definition of a devilish Luciferian force. Steiner would have considered almost all of the Hindu gurus devilish. The guru, in allowing his students to worship him, is in the end only rotting his own soul, entering ever more deeply into the control mechanism of the fields. Long-term, it doesn't do much for the student's spiritual journey, other than for a while relieving them of the burden of having to think.

As a metaphysical writer and commentator on spiritual ideas, I often wondered how modern teachers like the Hindus—who are the most into the caste system, snobbery, control, and entrapment—do so well. How is it that the modern gurus and authors who are the most into power, money, glitz, and control, manage to rise almost magically in spite of themselves? In spite of their wishy-washy, often inaccurate, or bogus message, and what is often a blatantly nefarious way of operating. It seems to me the worse or more evil a guru or teacher, the greater their power-base for control and financial gain.

I have met a lot of spiritual writers and teachers, and what I gradually discovered was that behind what is often a feigned goodness is a hidden darkness, or a downright evil character. Yet, one after the next, these adepts rose magically to a god-like status. I watched as this motley collection of pedophiles, misers, power-trippers, drug abusers, sex addicts who waffle on about family values, and financial manipulators, pretended to be squeaky clean. I watched as they cast their spells over the weak and needy. I wondered how the heck they got away with it. Furthermore, I couldn't understand how they could reasonably hide their darkness while blatantly accepting the living-god persona projected upon them by the faithful. Knowing much about the dark side of their lives, I wondered why they never got caught. Who or what is protecting them? But more than that, I wondered how it is that their crushing mediocrity is admired by so many. How did they come to control and influence so many? How did they get to superstar status overnight, almost as if by magic? Why does the media like them so much? Surely any fool can see that the guru is after status and money—you don't have to be a clairvoyant to work that out.

The answer lies in the fields upon fields. Each field has an identity just as your body has an identity. The nature of each field is to control, the same as it is the nature and function of your body to control its functions that are life sustaining. It is not concerned with how many microbes, viruses, or cells it kills off or rejects, or how many kilojoules of energy it consumes; its only concern is to sustain itself. The field around our planet is the same. It does not consider itself evil. It controls because it is in its nature to do so. Control grants it the security and illusion of immortality. If any part of itself seeks to individualize and do its 'own thing' it is automatically crushed, for it will threaten the field's raison d'être.

Each field of course has a dominant influence over ordinary people. Anyone who is even slightly insecure and therefore needs to manipulate or control, or anyone who exhibits even mild fascist tendencies, will be empowered by the field. Those who seek power, status, and elitism, and those who seek to manipulate, will automatically be empowered by what seems to be an invisible force. Hence, the magic that often surrounds mediocrity. Those who are congruent with the field's nature will rise magically to the top of their chosen field of endeavor. Be they a guru or a filmmaker. If you are not into setting yourself up over others, or you don't seek to feed off people or to control them, and if glitz, admiration, power, and money are not your trip, your career chances are very limited. Remember, the field only elevates whatever is congruent to power; everything else is crushed underfoot or marginalized. This might explain why you never got the breaks you hoped for. It may also explain why complete incompetents have risen to power over you. The discrimination of the field is merciless. It will broach no challenge to itself. In addition, it has forces on the ground in positions of control that mirror its needs exactly. So, for example, the mainstream media that waffles on endlessly about the freedom of the press will allow no such thing. You can say what you want as long as you agree with the status quo. Write an article that says that the printing of money is enslavement of the people, that tax is blatant theft, and that business monopolies should be abolished, then send it to the Herald Tribune and see how far you get. When politics are discussed on TV, government experts are given the bulk of airtime and the official opposition the rest. Try getting on if your stance is that the socialists and conservatives, Republicans and Democrats, are equally corrupt; that, in effect, the population would best be served if political parties were abolished. Go on to say that you feel the buying of favorable legislation via political donations ought to be outlawed and see if your ideas will ever find air on any mainstream discussion program. I think not.

The fields are spooky but the representatives of the field on the ground are even spookier. We see them in power, dominating day to day. They are sold to us every day as the logical, sensible expert—whose judgment shouldn't be questioned. Domination comes with a Cheshire Cat grin, a pinstripe suit, and a phony air of reasonableness. The Health Minister reassures us that Mad Cow disease is no danger to humans; the university professor states as a god-given fact that last week's floods are due to global warming. The economist tells us that the advent of the new Euro is a jolly good thing. The fact that the currency has fallen like a stone since its inception is ignored in the light of the wonderfulness of its uniformity.

The Sphere (the field) needs conformity to feed off humanity and to ensure that certain individuals remain empowered, especially those who would exercise extremes of power and control over us. So a non-entity like Adolf Hitler rises magically from nowhere to command all of mainland Europe. One could argue it was just a coincidence, but looking back you can see his rise to power was driven not by his charisma or his talent, for Hitler was mediocre to the extreme and a crushing bore, but by his knowledge of the satanic, left-hand path and his ability to tap 'the field.' He knew how to reach and appeal to the hidden forces deep within his people's collective unconscious. It was the occult nature of Hitler's journey and his ruthlessness that gave him the inner help he needed to take him to the top so quickly. There are probably 100,000 mini-Hitlers around today, rising up in their chosen field by using some of the very same techniques that Adolf used. I'm sure you have met a few, we all have.

It says in the Bible that at the end-time false prophets will rise up and enjoy great prestige and acclaim. I can't say I know what an end-time is. It may just mean the end of an era, as we move from Pisces to Aquarius, or it may mean the end of the world. Though I doubt the world will end anytime soon, although it may go through some major changes. Meanwhile, the 'false prophet' syndrome is everywhere. Not just with the sleazy TV evangelists and snake oil salesmen—alternative spirituality and the New Age is chock full of dodgy characters. Anyone who sets themselves up between ordinary people and God must by the nature of their action seek control. So that would make them, in Steiner's definition, a false prophet.

Of course, the false prophet makes his need for glitz, money, and power part of his immortality and therefore holy and good. Just as the tyrant sees himself as a kindly father figure, the pain he inflicts upon others is but part of the greater good. The Nazis shipped people to the death camps, convinced they were 'problem solving.' The alleged pedophile, slight-of-hand trickster, Sai Baba, who for many decades was considered by the dimwitted as a living-god, told the young boys he sexually abused that he was helping them on their spiritual path by raising their kundalini. I'm sure he believed what he told them.

It is the nature of the false prophets to cloak themselves in denial, explaining away bizarre actions with platitudes. The tyrant always finds a reasonable explanation. It's part of the way the Sphere operates, obfuscating and covering the truth. Dark becomes light, evil becomes good; the miser sees himself as generous and kind. The tyrant believes himself to be the benefactor and protector of the weak. The black magician sees himself to be in service to his ideals, which he believes are powerful, holy, and good. There is no self-regulation within the field for everything is clouded with a patina of distortion and lies. So the TV evangelist can endlessly bleed little people, using fear as the driving tool, promising to direct their requests toward God. He then does nothing but counts their money and composes yet another subtle manipulation for the following broadcast.

Of course, if we look closely, almost every organization, be it financial, social, political, or religious, has within it the propensity for Luciferian control. One must therefore differentiate between acceptable administration of human activity and manic control. As I said before, to administer a railway system is to set timetables and hire competent staff to keep the trains running on schedule. It's only when we see manipulation, threat, and the misuse of power, monopoly, covert deals, corruption, dishonesty, and the use of undue force that the administration of an activity becomes Ahrimanic or Luciferian.

If you begin to look at who controls the media, the printing of money, and the creation of debt, who has the monopoly over oil, gold, diamonds, and the financial markets; who writes the legislation of control; and who the arms manufacturers are, things get really spooky. It's almost always the same people. But let's leave that for a moment and look at something that is even stranger. This part of the story is where my particular expertise lies as I have spent 25 years trying to understand the etheric and the influence of the transdimensionals.

The transdimensionals are very much a part of the etheric field round Earth and they exist inside its Sphere as we do. Their issue is also control. They carry the message of the field to the minds of humankind and evolve as identities that are part of the field. Imagine them as a piece of a jigsaw puzzle. They have a distorted shape and so can only fit in one place in the overall jigsaw. Part of the jigsaw is the perverse nature of the human mind, so they bolt on to that, influencing control. They become a part of the human jigsaw and its evolution. They are part of the overall jigsaw (the Sphere) and they are locked into, and communicate with any human mind that is congruent, which of course is also in the Sphere as we all are.

9

Transdimensionals and the UFO Game

Let's begin at the beginning.

What is a transdimensional? The answer is, we don't know exactly because by their very nature they exist in etheric planes and those planes are hard to define and are not normally visible to the naked eye. A simple definition would be: a transdimensional is any intelligent evolution that permeates the earth plane but is not human, animal, or of the Earth. Transdimensionals are also all those evolutions that are not here, that don't permeate our plane of existence. Transdimensionals would include ghosts, all manner of nature spirits, the UFOs, the Greys, the Nordics, the Reptilians, Bigfoot, the Watchers, the Nefilim, and the Anunnaki (if they exist), the Flying Rods, and any other unnamed, unrecognized entity that is here but beyond our ken.

Let's kick off with the story of the UFOs as that is where most of the transdimensional spookiness appears on a daily basis. The first ever UFO wave of the modern era occurred around August/September 1946 in Europe. It wasn't until 1947 that the pilot of a small plane saw UFOs over Mt. Rainier in Washington State; it was he who coined the phrase 'flying saucer.' Now you may wonder what UFOs have to do with the fields and the on-the-ground controllers, but I hope to show you that they are part and parcel of the same thing.

Let me first say that, there is no evidence to suggest that UFOs are craft from other planets, or even other star systems, and there is only very circumspect and highly suspicious evidence to suggest they are solid, nuts-and-bolts craft. The way to work everything out is to proceed in the opposite direction to the flow of information, for the UFO scene is riddled with disinformation, as are crop circle investigations and other transdimensional conspiracy theories.

Think of this: if you wanted people to believe in solid UFOs, wouldn't the supposed crash at Roswell in 1947 work just perfectly? You deny there ever was a crash, and you offer some blatantly ludicrous explanation about hot air balloons that no one will believe. If people don't believe the government's explanation, then they have to believe in the crash. Throw in a couple of rednecks who swear blind their grandpa saw it all happen and bingo! You have pretty much got the story sorted.

From time to time you have to keep the BS alive, so enter Colonel Phillip Corso. A decorated veteran with a fine military record who writes a book called The Day After Roswell. In it he claims the 1947 crash was real and that he was assigned the task of collecting the technology that was recovered from the craft, which eventually led to the invention of night-vision goggles, the silicone chip, and fiber optics. He says it was his job to disperse the recovered technology among American industry, which explains why America has taken such a technological leap forward over recent decades. Pure and utter piffle.

When you sign the Official Secrets Act or any oath of secrecy, the best that can happen to you if you become a traitor is that you spend the rest of your days in the slammer. However, the most likely thing to happen is that you'll be pushing up daisies, six feet under. Security organizations do not piss about. My father was a highly decorated officer seconded to the intelligence service. He would have fallen off his chair laughing at the story. When Colonel Corso wrote the Roswell book, he was living on a cozy pension with all his perks: veteran's benefit, health benefits, blah, blah. While in his cozy cubbyhole he decides to risk everything and spill the beans, violating his oath of secrecy, and no one in the military takes a bit of notice. If Corso was really acting on his own without the permission of someone high-up he would have been picked up a long time before the book even went to press. Only two things are possible. The first possibility is highly unlikely, and it suggests that what Corso wrote was true and that someone in the military intelligence had asked him to put the record straight on his or her behalf, as they had been suddenly overwhelmed with pangs of righteousness. The second possibility, which is very much more likely, is that what Corso wrote about, the technology in the Roswell crash, was part of the ongoing solid-UFO disinformation campaign that the military want us to believe. Everyone who met Colonel Corso said he was a nice guy. He claimed he was never paid a dime in royalties for his book and that was probably right. He was fed the story and he followed orders as he had done all his life.

The famous video of the supposed autopsy on an alien being that had allegedly died in the Roswell crash was a further disinformation attempt; but it fell apart when the video was proven to be a fake. Of course, even though the video was bogus, it served its purpose. Many never realized it was a fake, and anyway, anything that confuses the issue becomes a valuable cog in the disinformation wheel. There have been recent, somewhat feeble attempts to revitalize the autopsy video as the real thing. It's amazing how the game's played.

Remember this, in spite of tens of thousands of sightings, photos, and now videos, including the famous UFO 'flotilla' videos taken in Mexico in the early 1990s, there has never ever been a photo of a UFO on the ground. The disinformation mill feeds out rumors that the US Air Force has got such photographs, but that is very unlikely to be true, and there is no known photo in private hands. Setting aside officer Lonnie Zamora's alleged on-the-ground sighting in New Mexico, there are very few reported sightings of UFOs on the ground. What does it tell you? A solid craft that transports extraterrestrials has to land some place every so often, otherwise there is no point to the craft. The UFOs don't land. Transporting entities from outer space to Earth is obviously not the UFOs purpose.

UFOs that are chased or followed by aircraft often display enormous bursts of speed, and they are often reported making right angle turns at an extreme velocity. A solid craft cannot stand that kind of strain, nor could any of its occupants, if they were made up of atoms and molecules. The force of gravity of a right-hand turn at thousands of miles per hour would kill them instantly.

The authorities want us to believe in nuts-and-bolts UFOs and solid occupants that mean us no harm. I am almost 100 percent sure that the UFO is in part, if not completely, an etheric phenomena. It may be possible that at a slow speed or at the lower end of the heat spectrum, the UFO shifts from etheric to semi-solid or even solid. But I doubt it. At slow speeds it may look solid but that does not mean it is solid. Instead, I think the UFO is a shape-shifting living entity, as are its various occupants: the Greys, the Reptilians, the Nordics, the flying orbs that are emitted from mother ships, colored lights, and so on.

A number of researchers have noticed that UFO shapes constantly change to fit the perceived leading edge technology of the day. In the late 1800s and early 1900s, UFOs looked like air balloons. During the war they appeared as phantom fighter planes called Foo Fighters. After the war, once Britain had experienced the V2 rocket attacks, UFOs started to appear as flying rockets. There was a spate of rocket-shaped UFO sightings over Scandinavia, especially in Sweden, where many rocket-style UFOs were seen to plunge into Swedish lakes. Interestingly, Sweden was neutral during the war. So the phony rocket show was just for them, as they would not have seen the German V2 rocket as a part of their war experiences.

It is important to remember that during the war, the Nazis had secretly developed a saucer-shaped flying craft called the Vril. So the first saucer-shaped UFOs in 1947 were just the next shape-shift to follow our technological advances. There are even more recent photos of modern UFOs where the craft have swastikas painted on them, which I find very interesting.

After the Americans landed on the moon in 1969 and the subsequent Apollo missions in the 1970s, we got used to seeing pictures on TV of astronauts wandering around collecting rock samples from the moon's surface. There followed a few rare, alleged, on-the-ground sightings of UFOs, where the occupants stood by their craft also studying rock samples. As usual no pictures were taken. The most famous of these sightings was again officer Zamora's sighting in New Mexico.

After the Americans developed their triangular stealth aircraft, UFOs changed from saucer-shaped to mainly triangular shaped. Huge, silent, flying triangles are the predominant UFO sighting of the current age. They are now seen on a daily basis somewhere in the world, usually in America or Europe. If tomorrow we suddenly invent flying telephone boxes, UFOs will appear as huge phone boxes flying about at lightning speed.

Of course, the whole UFO thing is complete bullshit. It's a control mechanism. The peek-a-boo nature of the UFOs' appearances is part of the ploy. They are deliberately mysterious in order to create in the minds of the observers the idea that mysterious solid 'higher' beings from other planets or star systems are here in great numbers, and that they have superior technology and a theoretical control over the laws of science and space/time. That idea is pure crap—disinformation. The legendary French UFO researcher, Jacque Vallee, figured it out. He wrote about the malevolent nature of UFOs in his classic book Messengers of Deception, which sadly is no longer available. Jacque Vallee has since bowed out of UFO research and is currently working at a university in Paris. The film Close Encounters of the Third Kind was Hollywood's story of his life. In fact, the film was another large dollop of disinformation. Hollywood seems to be a major source of UFO and ET disinformation; key players in Tinsel town must know about it. Obviously it suits them to follow instructions. It must be in their interests to do so. Spielberg's benign ET that likes children and just wants to return home is the most outrageous drivel ever offered. It is deliberately designed to confuse people and lower their guard. The occupants of UFOs are not benign. Far from liking children, they abduct them. UFOs are not from the stars, and unfortunately they are not going home. They are here to stay. Meanwhile, they will create as much fear and terror as they can.

The Sphere and the transdimensionals in it feed on many things, but the three things I have identified so far as etheric food for the field are: fear, noise (the human voice), and activity. The objective of UFO sightings and abductions is to fuel human intrigue and fear, as fear is food for the field. They control through people's fear as any good fascist organization might. Those who report having been abducted initially experience extremes of terror, but eventually, as they get used to the experience, their fear subsides. Often, they are then shown terrifying film footage of the world's future destruction, an ecological or nuclear holocaust, tidal waves, tsunamis, and asteroids hitting the planet, blah, blah. This fuels the terror for a while but eventually the abductee becomes blasé toward apocalypses. Once the abductee has absolutely no more fear about any of his or her transdimensional experiences, the abductions stop. No fear, no fuel for the field.

If you bear with me, I'm going to show you something that might make you puke with worry (just kiddin'); but I will also show you the escape hatch. They say ignorance is bliss. It is not. It's extremely bloody dangerous. It can be fatal for your soul. I can lead you to the truth of this with a degree of authority because I have endured years of extreme terror to discover the nature of the transdimensionals. It has not been an easy task, as the transdimensionals are very secretive. They don't want anyone knowing what is going on. But I was blessed with perception in this lifetime, and what I didn't get as a gift, I worked on myself to develop. I also had a lot of help— God's Gladiators. It was perception and the cat's curiosity that drove me forward to discover whatever I could. I didn't get the whole story as it's probably beyond my comprehension, and also, as I got closer and closer it became far too dangerous, so some of the story still remains hidden.

But from my experiences, I can say this: if there is one thing that will serve you more than anything else in this life, more than money, fame, or specialness, it is perception. It is the only currency of choice right now. When you pray to your God, don't pray for safety; pray for perception. Only the truly perceptive will ever be able to direct their lives to a healthy spiritual conclusion, which I am sure you deserve.

Now, here is something about the fields that is hard to comprehend and you may not want to believe. When Morpheus in The Matrix shows Neo the true nature of the fields, Neo cannot accept it. He flips out and starts shouting, "No. No." Then he throws up. Our whole human evolution is the puppet of a transdimensional force that is all around us. It controls everything. That force is not benign.

10

As Above, So Below

The transdimensionals in the sky above us are the same as the fascists that operate and control our world on the ground. Each operates in the same way—covertly. The transdimensionals terrorize people, hauling them away at night against their will, torturing them, indoctrinating them, and attempting to establish a psychological control over them. They are feeding on us from above and have another hidden agenda, what that is I can only surmise. The sad thing is transdimensionals reflect exactly the neo-Nazis that run the world on the ground. This is because they influence the neo-Nazis on the ground. The seemingly benign politician, in his pinstripe suit on the nightly news with a cheesy grin, masks his terrible vengeance upon humanity. He would swear blind that his intentions are for the greater good (the tyrant's excuse), and he will go to the grave believing his mind is his own, it is not. It was captured decades ago, when he first dreamed of power and control.

The control-trippers are driven from above. They in turn feed the Sphere from below. They are the field and it is also them. The field finds congruence inside their dark nature. The transdimensionals use that as a satellite dish to bounce impulses and ideas into other people's minds. Perpetual, insidious, often silent propaganda is beamed to us through thought transference. When a thought or an impulse comes to mind, how do you know it is you doing the thinking? You will imagine it is you because you may not have considered any other options. But the fact is, you don't actually know. If, for example, ideas enter your mind in French and you don't speak the language, you'd soon wonder who is doing the talking. But if an idea pops into your mind in your native tongue, in words and sentences that mirror the way you normally communicate, how can you tell who is doing the talking? I discovered as fact that one's mind is perpetually bombarded by the thoughts of others, especially thoughts that come from others of like mind, or those who are emotionally close to us. In addition, ideas also come in from the transdimensionals and elsewhere. We are constantly fed ideas, usually at our most vulnerable moments. Free will comes at a price— it ain't free.

So if an idea pops into your head to go next door and rape your neighbor, you don't know if that is your idea or if it has come from somewhere else. If you are an honorable, kindhearted, and easy going person, you'd reject the idea in seconds. But if you have shadow Nazi tendencies that are hidden, the idea might resonate and take hold and you will act it out. How many times do the courts hear a criminal say that at the time the crime was committed he or she had no idea how they could have acted in the way they did? The thought entered their mind during an emotional or vulnerable moment, and the next thing they knew they stabbed their granny without overriding the impulse.

The fields upon fields are all around us. We are like fish in the sea with no comprehension of what lies beyond where we live. The fish are, in a sense, controlled by the water and the conditions the seawater offers. If a fish could talk, it would describe seawater as a great benefit, but to an earthbound human looking in from a different dimension, it's obvious that the sea controls and limits the fish's potential. Furthermore, the sea is bloody dangerous for the fish. It is not aware of the danger. If the fish could wander on to the beach and hide in the bushes, it would be a lot safer.

When a fish is swimming in a shoal of fish and the shoal makes a sudden left turn, the talking fish might tell you it has made that decision, but in fact, it has only followed the morphic (information) field created by the shoal. That message was passed to all the members of the shoal by the overall field (seawater) and all the fish instantly turned left. Like water, the field around us is an excellent conductor of energy. It has almost no resistance. It must have zero mass, or almost zero mass. That is why a UFO can make a 90° left turn at high speed. The UFO is not solid, and it is moving in the field even though it looks to us like it is solid and it is flying through the air. Anytime the UFO decides to commit 100 percent to the field, it disappears from human view.

The fields upon fields are everywhere. In the air we breathe, in the ground below our feet, in the solid walls of our homes, in our actions, and our ideas. It's in our blood, our body, and our brain. In the same way that a killer shark is an extension of the field it lives in, the UFOs are predators of the field we live in.

Now, imagine a peaceful lagoon that is close to the sea but cut off from it by sandbanks. There are no predators in the lagoon and the seals and the fish that live there thrive and they are oblivious to any danger. Suddenly, conditions change and a high tide washes the sandbanks away; the lagoon is now connected to the sea. In some way, a way that is beyond the lagoon's aquatic inhabitant's comprehension, the lagoon, that is now an inlet, gives off a new signal. That signal is picked up by sharks out at sea and it takes them one year to make it to the inlet. Once they get there they are delighted to find an inlet teaming with food (energy). The good news travels out in the morphic field that is the sharks' inner communication and more and more show up. The sharks discover a strange fact. No matter how much of the energy of the inlet they consume, there is an ever-increasing explosion of inhabitants in the lagoon and lots of activity and sharks are attracted to blood and there is a lot of that in the lagoon. The human etheric version of fish blood is fear. The UFO feeds off fear and it goes out of its way to create it.

As I've said, before World War II, UFO sightings were very rare. Since the war they have become more common, to where they now occur on a daily basis. A number of UFO researchers all came to the same conclusion, more or less at the same time. They said the explosion of the first atom bomb was the etheric signal humanity gave off to attract UFOs. I think this idea came about because people who have been abducted by the buggy-eyed Greys have been shown films of nuclear explosions. The Greys give the abductee the impression that they are concerned about the safety of planet Earth. Yet the Greys see the earth plane as an energy source that they can use; there is no evidence that they are benevolent or that they care about the safety of humans, anymore than hunters care about animals in the forest. Often an abductee is shown a film snippet of a nuclear or ecological holocaust, and he or she is then told they are responsible for warning the rest of humanity. Excuse me? Ding! Ding! Seen this one before? Like on last night's news.

Here we go again, offering ordinary people global problems they can't fix. Is the abductee the Secretary General of the United Nations, a famous broadcaster, a political person, or part of the White House or Kremlin? No way! The abductee is called Hank and he works as a clerk at the 7-Eleven in Chattanooga, Tennessee. Giving Hank these 'save the world' instructions will serve to trigger his ego and confuse him. Of course, if there were an important message for humanity it wouldn't be given to Hank, who may be sweet but is totally unsuited for the job. You would give your important message to someone who had a bit of clout and credibility, Oprah Winfrey say, who could possibly do something about warning people of the holocaust problem.

So what does that tell you? It tells you people will believe whatever you feed them as long as you play to their self-importance. It tells you that the ecological or nuclear holocaust ain't happening any time soon, and no buggy-eyed Grey, nor your man Hank, is in the early warning business.

PARDON ME BOYS,
IS THAT THE CHATTANOOGA CHOO-CHOO?
HOLOCAUST TIME,
TRACK FORTY-NINE.

I don't think so. Sorry.

Now some say the atom bomb might have created a new hole in the Earth's etheric, allowing more UFOs into our dimension, but I don't think that fully explains the sudden arrival of the UFOs in 1946. Remember, the UFOs as Foo Fighters were tracking fighter squadrons from the beginning of the war, years before the bomb went off. Furthermore, the UFO and its inhabitants can read our minds. They would have known that the bomb was going to go off years before the explosion at Hiroshima—anyway I'm sure they were involved in its design and manufacture. The bomb was put together at an incredible speed by military scientists who hadn't even mastered simple stuff like radar. Excuse me! Ding! Ding! Got a bit of Reptilian (UFO) help, did they? The objective of the atomic bomb is not really to blow us up; it's to keep us scared.

No. I think we have to look for a UFO arrival explanation elsewhere. Remember, a UFO is at one level an etheric being, and its inhabitants are also etheric beings who exhibit fascist tendencies. The war created a lot of hate, not just the Nazis' hate but the Allies' hate as well, along with the Japanese army's extreme cruelty. Then there was the vengeance, some of it expressed, some of it unexpressed. The world was awash in hate and fear for six years. It was the world's shadow made manifest and it was that body of energy that brought the UFOs in. The bomb may have created a bit of attention, as 150,000 people being fried in agony would be something the UFOs would want to watch and be a part of. But it wasn't the reason they suddenly came in such great numbers. They came for the food. The plat du jour? Hate, agony, distress, and fear.

The destruction of 150,000 unarmed civilians at Hiroshima and Nagasaki were acts of hate and vengeance. Initially, the bombings were explained as necessary as American lives would have been lost in the taking of Japan. It was only later that it became known that the Japanese Emperor Hirohito had already agreed to surrender before the bombs went off. Truman's order to drop the bombs on Japanese civilians came out of his deep-rooted hatred of humanity. It was his megalomaniac desire to exercise a god-like power that granted a horrible, unnecessary death to 150,000 unarmed civilians just as a show of strength. The show of strength was not just for the benefit of the Japanese; it was for the whole world. Look at this demonic bullshit everyone. We control your life. We are the supreme authority. We can fry you in seconds. It would be terrifying to contemplate where Truman is today. The sad part about his acts is they remain in the books of American karma as a debit. So Truman has lumbered innocent Americans with an upcoming disaster. Those film clips of Truman wisecracking—a cheery little fellow in silly clothes, playing golf—masked a covert Nazi, one who was no different to his opponents. The world was certainly a better place once Brother Harry quit the earth plane.

After 1946, the UFOs began their war to establish control of the human dimension. It's a two-pronged move: there are those on the ground (humans) and those in the air. Remember, the UFOs are Nazis as are the Grey drones and the Nordics. The blond, perfectly featured Arian types seem to be in command of the Greys. While the UFOs are sometimes seen to fly in daylight, the Greys almost always operate at night. They can't hack the light—they often smell of sulfur and are devilish to the extreme.

Just like the Nazis, they haul people away against their will and torture them. Sometimes the individuals are subjected to sexual abuse and rape by the transdimensionals. Abductees talk about the breeding programs that the Greys seem to conduct, which involves taking ova and sperm from abductees and attempting to create life. The Nazis had the same shoddy programs of eugenics, in which they tried to breed a master race of Arians (Nordic looking folk) by whittling out any deformities or genetic weakness, and killing those who didn't fit their genetic blueprint. The Greys are pretending; pretending to act out the same kinds of experiments the Nazis performed.

The Nazis ruled with surveillance and terror. The UFOs do the same. They are watching all the time. The Nazis used disinformation, propaganda, and trickery. The UFOs use the same control mechanism, creating the illusion that they are the supremely powerful. Hitler used indoctrination and mass hypnosis to mesmerize the crowd. The transdimensionals do the same with their acrobatic displays, and through their on-the-ground allies and the media's denial of them. Remember, denying them is a ploy to get people to see UFOs as mysterious and all-powerful.

What is the media? It is the voice of the world controlled by a very small number of people. Its function is to drip-feed fear into the minds of ordinary people. If you believed what you saw and read, you would imagine yourself powerless. You would also give away your individuality, as the media endlessly repeats that the subjugation and enslavement of the individual is for the greater good. The buggy-eyed Greys say exactly the same thing, telling the abductee, "Sorry, this is going to hurt a bit, but it's for the greater good."

Look at the nightly news and as the broadcaster speaks, mentally finish his or her secret unspoken sentences. What are they actually reporting? What remains unsaid? Everything. What remains secret? All of it. They fed you the Grand Lie, the unspoken lie, which, of course, follows the spoken lie that states all is well and that those in power are benign and have our interests at heart. That which is announced on TV with great fanfare is said to be true. But it's never the truth. It can't be. If those in power admitted that they were deceiving the population and robbing them blind, people would react. So the President announces belt-tightening measures to reduce the deficit, programs are cut, and he waffles on about the need for everyone to pull their weight and pay their fair share in taxes. But he doesn't mention that the American government has 35 trillion dollars stashed away. The whole GDP of the US is just over three trillion dollars a year, so the Government has the entire US economy's turnover for 12 years in its secret coffers. The government could give every working person a $100,000 each and hardly dent the total it has stashed away. Plat du jour? More lies, control, higher taxes, belt tightening, less social programs, more restriction for ordinary people, and more and more power for the elite.

Recently in England, there was a very crippling strike of petrol delivery drivers, who were protesting the exorbitant taxes on fuel and diesel, which increased the cost of fuel to the British by 400 percent. The tax they pay is almost twice that which is gouged from other

Europeans. The Chancellor of the Exchequer got on TV and said that if fuel taxes were lowered the government would not be able to run the hospitals or pay old age pensions. It was a blatant lie, pure disinformation. The public support for the strike collapsed. At the time the slimy Chancellor Brown broadcasted the 'we'll run out of money lie,' the Treasury had billions of pounds in surplus that it wouldn't admit to, as well as the billions of pounds in surplus that is stashed away. The role of the media is to control, to scare, and to parrot whatever the government wants. If you don't want to be a victim of that, turn off the TV and don't buy papers.

YOU WILL NEVER BE FREE OF THE FIELD
UNTIL YOU REMOVE THE MEDIA FROM YOUR LIFE.

The control is of course political and social but more than anything else it's Ahrimanic. Its function is to disempower, misinform, and mislead people into making approved decisions. At first, it is impossible for us to comprehend what is going on. How can our kindly newsreader, who we see every night, who we know and trust, be part of a disinformation programming system? The fact is, he is. He's on top wages and he reads whatever is put in front of him. He wouldn't have the time or the resources to check the facts he is about to read. In reading the news, he spins manufactured ideas, official propaganda, and goo-goo speak into truth. Have you ever wondered why newsreaders hardly ever change? The same person is on TV every night for decades. Newsreaders go on forever because that is their strength. Once you see them over and over, and become familiar with them, they sound reasonable. It's like chatting to an old friend, you believe what you are being told and you don't ask questions. That is the function of news, lulling people into accepting a 'manufactured reality' that describes our world in the official, 'approved' way.

It's control for control's sake. The living nightmare that is deep inside the fat controllers is the Ahrimanic; they are trapped by it and want it externalized and made manifest. They want the prisoner-of-war camps. They want to be the voice of the world and will not allow anyone into the media unless they are benign or correspond to the same Ahrimanic feeling. The American, Noam Chomsky is one of the world's great thinkers. He is a dissident. He's the American equivalent of Sakarov. He wrote a great book called Manufacturing Consent, in which he talks about the manipulation of the population by the media. I read an article he wrote where he said he had been deliberately excluded from the media, and that he had only been on mainstream TV once in 15 years for a total of six minutes. It is impossible for ordinary people to understand how doctored their information is to suit the forces of control.

Let's go back to the Sphere. Its nature is control. The voice of the world is effectively silenced. No one is allowed to speak out against the fat controllers. Meanwhile, fear is drip-fed daily to the masses. The lies become the truth, and the real truth is buried. Any contradiction is considered heresy.

What else does the Sphere and the transdimensionals need? Activity—it/they feed on activity. The energy you spend rushing around day to day, helps to keep the Sphere and the transdimensionals going. How do the media define and sell activity. As a good thing? People must work and produce and be responsible, we are told. The unemployed need reeducation. You can't be healthy unless you run around. Go-getters are admired. Workaholics are good people who provide for their families. Sportspeople who rush around a lot are sold to us as superhuman. Overall, one could summarize the propaganda message as saying: action is good, inaction is slothful and not to be desired.

How do you ensure that everyone rushes around like chickens with their heads cut off? First, you sell them on 'Action Man' as an idea that is holy and good—he's got a Porsche and a pretty bimbo by his side. He's rushing about, life's a blast. He doesn't have to be feeling or sensitive, as long as he has lots of orgasmic experiences. They let you know he's in heaven. Next, you spoon-feed the ladies the same bullshit. She's the modern miss, the tough career woman juggling life, the kids, the period pains, the job, the mortgage; she's the one who has made it to consumer heaven in a man's world—against all odds. These action-oriented people are high achievers and they are sold as special and god-like. We are told they are happy. They have achieved a phony immortality through activity. No one is allowed to question the religion of activity.

How do you make absolutely sure that these people keep rushing about and that no one suddenly sells them on anarchist ideas like sitting on the porch whittling a stick? Easy. You take half their wages as tax so that no one thinks about finishing early, like Wednesday lunchtime say. In fact, make sure they have to do heaps of overtime just to survive. To ensure activity, you have to enslave the people, and the easiest way to do that is to control their money. This was achieved in America by the illegal founding in 1913 of the Federal Reserve. A private corporation mostly owned by Jewish families, most who originate from Europe. The chief moneymaking function of the Federal Reserve is to print worthless paper that then becomes real money overnight. That previously worthless paper is then lent at interest to American taxpayers.

I imagine that you understand how you are being enslaved to this racket, but here is a short story to show how this crime is perpetuated and why it is so clever.

Imagine a small village that operates only on barter; they have no currency or coins. The villagers realize that if they had a common currency, their economy would benefit as trade would be easier and thus would increase. Along comes a dude from the Federal Reserve Money Printing Company and says, "We'll give you currency and even put a drawing of the village chief's head on the notes." "Wonderful," say the villagers.

The Feds print a million dollars and deliver it to the villagers who sign for what was yesterday worthless paper—now they owe the Feds a million. They have also agreed to pay six percent interest a year for the loan of the money. Of course, it is a trap. The Feds have not printed enough money for the villagers to pay back its interest.

If there was one million dollars printed and it was lent to one village at six percent per year, and if they never spent the money on anything but dutifully paid the $60,000 a year in interest owed, at the end of 16.33 years they would have no currency left, as it would have all been returned to the Federal Reserve in interest. But they would still owe the Reserve the initial one million dollars. It's a trick. They can never repay the loan. To service the debt in the 17th year they would have to give the Feds part, or all, of the village. Of course, the Feds initial outlay to print the million dollars in notes that they gave the village was about $20,000. Now they have all the notes back, which they can lend to Village #2 while they gradually repossess all the wealth of Village #1, which is now in default. In another 16.33 years they can start repossessing Village #2. In the end, all the money and all the property of any village that falls for this trick is bound to wind up with the Federal Reserve Money Printing Company. Over a long enough timeline the Feds will wind up owning the world. Their outlay for owning everything is just the cost of printing. The cost is even less for the billions created via Federal Reserve Notes, or the money they create via computers as 'new' money that enters the system when it is credited to the accounts of institutions as loans.

Of course, the villagers didn't keep the money they borrowed stashed away. In fact, they dug a well and built a hospital and a new road, and so they went broke a long time before the 16.33 years were up. In the meantime, the workers had to do lots of overtime to create wealth to pay taxes so the village could pay interest to the Feds' printing company on what was never anything but phony paper (wealth). What the poor villagers never realized was, if they had bought a printing press, printed their own money, and distributed it among their inhabitants, there would have never been any interest due and instead of everyone working 50 hours a week so they could pay the foreigners at the Federal Reserve, they could have had exactly the same wealth for 25 hours of work a week.

The Federal Reserve hired some very nasty policemen to make sure taxes were collected, activity was kept up, and interest paid regularly. This caused a lot of stress and some villagers died. Others couldn't cope. They took drugs. Families broke up and violence, previously unheard of, broke out. Some villagers took to thieving from others to make ends meet. Now the village had to go to the expense of hiring their own policemen to keep law and order. It wasn't long before the villagers began to give up, and as they did they fell even more behind until eventually all the wealth of the village wound up with the Federal Reserve and the villagers died of sorrow.

This is the horrible trick played upon taxpayers year in and year out. The Reserve never prints or creates enough debt-free money to pay the interest that is due to them. So, if there is say one million dollars printed and the interest on that is $60,000 per year, there is no extra $60,000 with which to pay the debt. Even if at the end of the year, you could return the million dollars unspent, where would you get the extra $60,000 you owed the Reserve in interest? They only printed the million, not the million plus the interest due—it is Shylock demanding and receiving his pound of flesh through trickery. It's a heinous crime against humanity by folk who are sub-human. If you think it is not sub-human, the Sphere has you in its propaganda, or you haven't understood properly.

Now you can't use previously printed money to pay the interest that is due as that also owes unavailable interest. The only thing that can happen is that the interest owed gets rolled over to create even more debt, or that the interest has to be paid in goods, not money. So you will have to use real estate, gold, diamonds, shares, and valuables to pay the interest, but not money, as there is no money available with which to pay it. So, as I've said, the debt can never be paid. It accumulates until the Reserve owns the world.

How can anyone with even a modicum of decency perpetuate such a terrible torture upon ordinary people? These fascist manipulators must hate their fellow men and women with a vengeance. They must gloat over how cleverly they illegally tricked the American people and the rest of the world into financial slavery. Meanwhile, hundreds of thousands of Americans drop dead every year under the stress of it all. It's another Harry Truman Hiroshima all over again. It doesn't matter how many people die, how many families crack up, or how many drift to helplessness and despair, just as long as the Feds wind up owning the world. They have trillions stashed away that they can move around in secret to sustain the political and commercial interests of the owners—there is no legal way of controlling or scrutinizing their activity.

Where is the media in all of this? Protesting on behalf of the villagers? Hell no.

The media sticks the ghoulish Chairman of the Federal Reserve Money Printing Company up on TV several times a week. The New York Times and the Herald Tribune are on the same side as the Federal Reserve and write cheery articles about him. They sell him as a good guy. One who is dutifully managing the villager's economy, ensuring that inflation stays under control, and generally keeping an eye on the books and a tight rein on spending. It's all backwards, remember?

Phew! That's good news. For a moment I thought the craggy bastard was killing more Americans each year than all those who died in the Vietnam War. You mean he's not breaking up families, sowing seeds of violence and despair, and delivering mayhem to the working people? Phew! It's such a relief to know he's helping us. For a second there, I felt he was no different to the rest of the Nazis who control the world: heartless, mean, cruel, and a terrible liar. "No," says the media. "He's helping you little villagers." "Jeez," we say, "Praise the Lord, we're truly blessed."

The villagers had two chieftains: Abraham Lincoln and John Kennedy. Both realized this phony money scam eventually forced people into a hidden slavery. They saw it was making people sick. They decided in their great wisdom that the village should pay back any phony money owed and henceforth print their own interest-free money. Both chieftains, I'm sorry to say, were assassinated before they could implement the plan that would have liberated the villagers forever. The people who own this racket are powerful, and the field will never allow the villagers to escape anyway, not until the field itself is destroyed. That is because the humans who print phony money run the media, control our financial institutions, and enact crippling legislation upon us, are the embodiment of the field. They are the Sphere and its reason d'être is enslavement, monopoly, and control.

This is awfully hard to accept. Everyone looks so reasonable. The arguments are so logical. There are no counter arguments, or if there are they are dismissed as illogical or fanciful. What is hidden underneath? Perpetual activity, which is made to seem holy and good. Activity brings wealth (half of which is taken from you— sorry, sorry); the rest will bring you happiness, so they say. It's a lie, a big lie. It's a scam to keep you active and the fat controllers, who are beyond the law and beyond the everyday stress of life, in power and in control over us. Remember this, activity is a fear avoidance mechanism. It's the way people who feel scared avoid the feeling. Of course, if the system was not based on fear (food), you wouldn't need so much activity (more food). This is why the system sells fear and activity drip by drip by drip—to feed off the fear and the activity they know the fear will generate. Knickers! Refuse to be scared in this lifetime, fuckin' refuse! And remember there is an escape hatch, and there are lots of good men and women around to help you. Learn to trust good men and women. Don't be suspicious. When your feelings say trust this one, follow along. Cautiously at first if you must, but follow. In the end the field will fall apart. Help is here.

MEANWHILE, REMEMBER,
YOU CAN NEVER ESCAPE
THE FIELD UNTIL YOU REMAIN STILL—
NEVER.

What else does the field feed on? Noise. It needs lots of noise. The noise it needs is that generated by the human voice. No problem. We'll have to look to our friends in the media to help us. Give us lots of free noise. TVs and radios blaring, ghetto blasters, CDs, DATS, minidisks, Walkmans, sound systems at home, in the car, in shops, in the elevator, in hotel lobbies, in the toilet—everywhere, endless noise. And don't forget mobile phones—make sure people can talk, talk, talk, anywhere, anytime. Just make sure noise runs 24 hours a day, non-stop. Make sure it's a perpetual cacophony of madness. When there is constant noise people cannot think properly or ask awkward questions, nor can they properly perceive. We need noise to feed the field, so get our pals in the media to make sure there is an endless supply of free noise. Make people who specialize in noise—heavy metal bands, singers, rappers, and so forth into national heroes. That should confuse the fuck out of everyone.

You will never escape the field—never—until you learn that your power is in silence.

What else sustains the field? Partially what else sustains the field might be described as pleasure—the pleasure it has in the control it exercises. So, for example, if you were someone who liked to gloat over control, you'd be a camp guard, and as you stood in your turret, with your special uniform on and a gun over your shoulder, you would gaze down on the prisoners and revel in the warped pleasure of knowing that you had the power of life and death over people. That it was you who was creating the custodial hell of the prison. It was you who ensured people remained trapped and incarcerated. You would get a pleasure from that if that is the kind of person you are.

The field finds a pleasure in its own order: order is intrinsic to the dynamics of the field. It's not order, as we understand it, like say, books in a row on a shelf. It's the religion of control, because control is how the field seeks to ensure its immortality. It is the way it makes believe it will exist forever; it's how it sustains its life, its energy, and its vitality. In addition, the field is aware of the entities evolving inside it, so, as I said, the shark is in the sea and the sea moves through the gills of the shark and gives it life. The shark is the sea and the sea is the shark. They are part of the same dimension. Seawater has no desire to control. In fact, it is controlled by an external force, the moon. But if seawater were into control, it would enjoy the shark's abilities. It would like the fact that sharks were policing, controlling, consuming, and terrorizing the seal and the fish that lived there. It would enjoy that because it would be an extension of how the field feeds its immortality. The sharks would in turn be empowered by the field and they would act according to their control trip.

Our minds are influenced by transdimensional forces that drip-feed slime into our consciousness. They feed us ideas, attempting to influence the course of events while hoping to establish control, creating the illusion that there is a supreme power over people. In the same way, a government creates the illusion that it has power over you. It has no power but it suits it to create the illusion that it does. The police are the same. They create the illusion that they are wandering around keeping things in order. The police cannot keep order; the citizens agree to be orderly. Any time 50 million people decide to be disorderly, the police are completely fucked and so are the military. Their power is a complete illusion.

The transdimensional influence is expressed as insecurity and nastiness, cruelty and greed. If you are a good person, if control is not your racket, if you do not manipulate or exercise terror over others, then the nastiness of the field cannot influence you a great deal. But it can still influence you to a certain extent. Let's talk some more about mind control, programming, and brainwashing, and how the racket works.

These transdimensional entities are here to dominate the world. In 1947 there wasn't a great quantity of them, and they didn't have a lot of power because they didn't have a lot of energy. The advent of the Nazis brought them in in greater numbers. They are one and the same. Since humans have evolved and become more plentiful and more active once the programming took control via the development of mass media, the field has grown enormously. These entities are here to trap the souls of the world, so after noise and communication became global, entrapment became easier.

I have to tell you something that I find exceptionally sad. They have done a good job. It's easy to trap people as they are weak and predictable. Most people on Earth are never going to get out, they can't escape. They are too indoctrinated. They are too much into control, fear, materialism, money, hatred, and anger. They are too small, they are victims of the field without realizing it—they are the field and the field is them. The number of people who could escape the field is dwindling with every passing day. This is not a good thing for the future of humanity, but it is part of our long-term evolution. We are in the inlet and we are trapped. The only thing that can escape the inlet is a fish or a seal that isn't scared of sharks—one that can leave the so-called security of the inlet, which isn't secure anyway. One that isn't scared of thinking differently, that isn't scared to be silent, that isn't scared to be on its own, that isn't scared to identify within itself its own reality and live and die by it. Only those who have that kind of power will ever get away.

We are trapped and yet we are not trapped. A man or a woman who develops perception, who has individuality (which is, after all, true spirituality), and one who has nostalgia for eternity, can make a run for it and beat the sharks. The sharks are actually helpless against the power of an individual; but powerful when they have the entire mechanism of the field behind them, programming people into powerlessness. In our world, the field enjoys itself, and the people of the field, the fat controllers, those who own everything—Hollywood, big business—are thrilled to be as important as they are. They like the perks, the specialness, and the wealth. They like the fact that they can elevate one person and reject another. They enjoy the power trip. They live in hell but find it comfortable because prestige, status, and money make it comfortable on a purely material or social basis. The field wants to be the supreme power. It wants to be God just as the shark at the entrance of the inlet wants to be God and to dominate all the fish and seals that live in the lagoon. But we can get away and that is the amazing part of this story. We can get away in spite of the fact that all these people are pitted against us, in spite of the fact that they seem reasonable when they appear on TV in their three-piece suits, and in spite of the fact that they sometimes exhibit warmth and kindness. Rarely, but sometimes. In spite of the propaganda, they are in fact Nazis. Sometimes they are mini-Nazis and sometimes they are full-blown Nazis, but they are Nazis nonetheless.

II

TRAPPED EARTHBOUND
SPIRITS IN THE ETHERIC

Here is something I found fascinating. Thirty years ago I was told by an initiate, who was the very best in his day, that many of the Jews who died in the camps during World War II were not able to escape the earth plane. He said that Hitler knew how to trap them. It was the first time I was ever introduced to the idea that for some there may be no way out. Previously, I presumed that everyone made it to either a heaven or a hell of some sort. In fact, part of hell (there may be other parts of hell I don't know about) is here in the etheric, inches away from your body. In the etheric, there are loads of earthbound spirits.

When you die, you have a small but reasonable opportunity to leave this dimension. If you cannot detach from your attachment to physical things; if you are manically into control; or if you have untoward tendencies (a darkness within you), it will be hard or impossible for you to leave. To leave, there is a wormhole that you fall down. I've seen it a number of times. I've even looked down it, and on occasions I have found myself at the other end of it. It seems that at death, the wormhole will not allow you to pass through unless you get there quickly. If you hang around too long, or if you are scared to let go and leave, you're stuck. In fact, you were trapped by your beliefs and attitudes a long time before you died. If you don't believe in life after death, if you commit suicide, or if you die a violent or sudden death, it will hamper your chances of escaping the earth plane—but it doesn't negate your chances completely. It has a lot to do with your individuality and personality, and how deep your nostalgia for God is.

Hitler knew how to trap the dead in the Sphere—many of his victims didn't get away. Hitler was one of the greatest devilish masters that ever lived, an occult master of the dark side. He could have been one of the greatest saints, but he chose to go the other way. He was taught by the best of European occultists. Hitler had unseen helpers. He was able to trap millions of Jews partly because they didn't believe in life after death, partly because many were killed so suddenly, and partly because many of the wartime ghetto Jews believed what the

German Nazis themselves did. When you look at it, it's quite alarming. I had a terrible time getting my head around this one when the Gladiators first showed it to me. I had difficulty comprehending it. I refused to see that the victims and the criminals had the same agenda, the same beliefs. It was a shock. I had been programmed to ignore the similarities.

The Nazis believed themselves to be members of a supreme race; the Jews also believed that they were a supreme race. The Nazis felt they were especially chosen by God to dominate the world. Their central theme was the idea of the Arian superman, selected by God. The Jews believed that they were special and chosen— that they were chosen by God to inherit the Earth. The Nazis did not believe in breeding outside their own kind, they insisted on genetic purity; the Jews also believe/d in genetic purity. They are not allowed to marry outside their gene pool. Hitler referred to the Jews as cattle. The Jewish law, the Torah, refers to non-Jews as goyim, which means cattle. It is permitted under Jewish law to kill the goyim, who are considered subhuman. A Jew is also permitted under his law to pillage and remove the property of the goyim. It is not a sin under his religious code. Killing people and removing their property was also permitted under Nazi law—the Nazis were autocratic, they liked control for control's sake. The Jews' religion is rather similar; it has over 600 mind-boggling laws to be followed. The Nazis were racists and against minorities. The ghetto Jews were racists, and they were not keen on the Africans either. The Nazis invented weapons of mass destruction, improving germ warfare delivery systems, and developing the V2 rocket. The wartime Jews (aided by the transdimensionals) invented Truman's vengeance—they gave us the atom bomb and the nuclear bomb and later the neutron bomb. Nazis, helped by the Allies to escape from Germany, ran much of the nuclear program in America in the early days after the war. My father's job after the war was to help German and Russian scientists escape from the Communist block. He'd enter East Germany undercover and help them escape to America.

The Nazis destroyed Jewish communities and forcibly shipped people into ghettos and camps. For 50 years the Israelis have bulldozed Arab homes forcing citizens into refugee camps, while not paying compensation for property seized. The Nazis didn't like paying compensation either. Of course, the ideas of racial purity—the chosen people, the superman destined to inherit the Earth—are all bogus. What is extremely odd is that the wartime Jews and the Nazis held many of the same ideas. When you look at it, it is bizarre to the extreme. It's amazing that no one has seen it before. It shocked me when I was shown it. I couldn't really accept it. At first, I thought it an anti-Semitic rant, but then I saw it for what it was, a statement of fact. The Nazis and the wartime Jews are two sides of the same elitist coin, like it or not.

What's even more bizarre is that the UFOs mirror the Nazis and they have even been seen to fly swastikas as insignia. I don't know if Hitler's mother being Jewish had something to do with his hatred. And anyway, it doesn't alter the fact that six million ordinary people were killed, which is terribly sad. Still, I found it very freaky when I saw that the victims and their tormentors had the same beliefs.

You can see that anyone who is born thinking they are special, believing they are genetically superior and chosen by God to be the master race, must, by their very nature, be a part of the field. They are the shark. These people are permitted by the laws they create to kill anyone who is not like them, and they can legally pillage whatever they want. You can see how these types, be they Nazis, wartime ghetto Jews, the Federal Reserve, or any tin-pot modern fat controller, have tendencies that were/are very akin to the field. When they try to escape this plane after death, they won't be able to. They won't have the velocity. They have already been trapped by their ideals, their materialism, their hate of humanity, their phony sense of specialness—all of which is very Ahrimanic. "We are the Chosen Ones; we are the god-like ones. We are here to own everything and to control and dominate everyone."

This isn't just a wartime Jewish thing, millions are now trapped: the real Nazis, modern neo-Nazis, tyrants, control-trippers, financial sleight-of-hand merchants, the phony prophets, the bent lawgivers, and so on. The study of control is painful for it is the study of nastiness. I realized, as have others before me, like Steiner, that the Ahrimanic control on the ground, inflicted upon us day to day, reflects a Luciferian dark control in the close-by etheric forces, and vice versa. I will expand on this later, but for the moment think of it like this: anyone good or benevolent who dies automatically drifts away from the earth plane—they have no need for material things or control. He or she finds themself in a spiritual world that reflects their warmth, openness, love, and goodness. It was their spiritual qualities that carried them away from the earth plane at death. However, the tyrants, the religious control freaks, the Chosen Ones, are stuck here, they can't get away. So eventually, over decades, a dark band surrounds us, which is the neo-Nazi sludge at the bottom of the spiritual septic tank of human evolution. As the sludge develops in the nearby etheric it becomes harder for ordinary people to break away after death— the noose tightens. Love is liberation. Loving people is setting them free; controlling them is satanic and entrapping. We need love so badly; without it we are trapped. Meanwhile, control on the ground is closing in on us. It's a two-pronged attack: you can watch from the bleachers or you can watch from the skies. It's the same game. Played by the same people. As above, so below. Ding! Ding! When I worked this out, and I had a lot of other world help to do so, I freaked.

PEOPLE KNOW WHAT IS GOING ON
AND THEY PRETEND IT'S NOT HAPPENING.
FEIGNED NAIVETY IS A FORM OF DENIAL.

Public records show certain groups of people having developed a commercial, political, or legal stranglehold over humanity. Look at how political contributions affect the flow of legislation. Or watch the effect that bent lawyers and shady judges have on the dispensing of justice. Everyone seems busy controlling something. The powerful Arab families control the production of oil. Jewish families control Hollywood and much of the Western media. They also have a monopoly over the trading of gold and diamonds, and they control financial markets via the Federal Reserve, which controls and profits from the printing of the world's major currency, the US dollar. It is the Federal Reserve that has enslaved the American worker. Now don't get confused between ordinary Jews, many of whom may be good people, and the controlling families. It's the same relationship between ordinary Christian people and the controlling elite of the Christian world. It's not a racist or religious thing, it's the ordinary people versus the controlling elite, be they Arab, Jewish, or the British aristocracy.

The game of the elite is pillage and control. An all-powerful, non-elected council of no particular denomination or race has been appointed to govern Europe. The idea of a European super state run by a supreme council was a cherished plan of Adolf Hitler's. It's a Nazi concept that he wrote about in Mein Kampf in 1924. It took 70 years to come about, but as the fascist band around us strengthens, eventually all of Hitler's ideas will be enacted into legislation. Hitler never went anywhere. He and his followers are alive and here in the close-by etheric.

Hitler's ideals are never more than a few inches from your left or right ear. Pick whichever one you fancy. You can choose the light or the dark. The dark is too close for comfort in my view. The light drifts away because it is into love and love liberates. It's geographic: the dark stays close to the demonic nature of the earth plane and the light drifts away, leaving us etherically surrounded by dark crud—sad but true.

Looking further a field, you can see that various despots have captured bits of Africa, Asia, and the Middle East, which they run as their private fiefdoms—Singapore and Kuwait, for example. World trade is captured and regulated by various agreements (NAFTA, GATT, and so on) that have put the Western workers on the dole and enriched the multinationals. Medicine is controlled by a handful of pharmaceutical companies, and doctors are given strict guidelines of which drugs to prescribe for various ailments. If a doctor deviates from prescribing the recommended drug, he or she may be dragged up before the Medical Board to explain their action. It's very scary, and career threatening, for a doctor to deviate from the drug-dishing control of medicine. He can do it every so often but he had better have a good explanation. If he or she does it more than once or twice, his career is over. It's a huge disincentive for a doctor to use his own judgment. Dishing out the 'approved' drugs is the safest way to go.

The power of absolute control is exercised over all human activity. Only the elderly can remember how free life used to be. Before the war there was very little legislation and low taxes, and though our economies were smaller and poorer, people were under much less pressure. If you had a British passport you could go and live anywhere in the world, there were no visas or immigration controls. There was also no police state, not in the Western world anyway, and there was no electronic surveillance or two million CCTV cameras watching the population, as there are in Britain today. An Englishman going about his lawful activity appears on CCTV on average 12 times a day. You see, this is not a racist or religious issue; it is an issue of domination over humanity. Since the war, the world population has increased, and as power and control became more and more absolute, it naturally bred more tyrants, who later became trapped in the nearby etheric world after death. It is partly a numeric thing and partly because subtle tyranny is much more common today. The dark powers that developed in the nearby etheric plane are between us and the spiritual worlds, between us and God. It's strong now. It will not let you through. Its idea is to trap you spiritually and never release you.

If you tell ordinary people that the world-mind is powerfully influenced by a fascist based transdimensional plane, they may consider you quite mad. Or the thought police will show up whispering lies as truth; swearing no such thing exists. But an ordinary person, even if they are well educated, usually has almost zero perception. They will have knowledge and facts and worldly experience, but they will not really believe in an extrasensory world. It suits them to say it doesn't exist. It's safer that way, because if they admit to it then they might have to look at the flimsy nature of their own BS. They will not have 'eyes' to see. They will ridicule the idea of etheric worlds. They have been programmed to deny the existence of the real fat controllers (or accept it). Ding! Ding! Even psychics and sensitives who counsel and assist others, often have only a very rudimentary perception of the true nature of these transdimensional worlds. Very few understand where these thoughts come from—they believe all thinking is self-generated. Naivety is often a form of denial.

The sky-people's influence is so much more than we ever imagined. Plus, what is so strange is that the UFOs and transdimensionals around this planet are sustained and enhanced by the people who died during the war and all the tyrants who have died since. Those dead souls exist in a nearby etheric hell that is part and parcel of the tightening band of control that forms a spiritual noose around the Earth.

I know that this idea may sound odd, but, as I said, I have studied etheric worlds for 25 years and I share and talk about the things that I have personally experienced over and over. I have since taught others to see it. When I talk about something I have not experienced, or something that I am not sure of, I am careful to offer it up for consideration, as an idea to think about. I don't state it as fact. Yet, I can say without fear of contradiction that the skies around us are littered with UFOs and transdimensionals, tens of thousands of them, maybe more, and they are linked both to the fat controllers on the ground and to the souls of the trapped dead in the etheric plane. How this alliance actually holds together in the construct of the Sphere, I cannot say precisely. The nature of it is still unfolding to my perception—and don't forget that they are doing their best to keep it hidden. The fat controllers on the ground also keep everything well hidden or muddled. The whole system operates that way.

The first time I ever saw the sky people, as I call them, was in the autumn of 2000. A sword-shaped contrail appeared in the sky. What was odd was, the vapor trail of the sword was quite low. It was not at the height one normally sees vapor trails as planes fly over. Also, I didn't hear the sound of a plane passing overhead. The other highly strange thing was, the vapor trail never broke up or moved in the wind. It sat along a ridge at say 10,000 feet and never changed shape. It was as if it had been fixed in the sky in some way.

It was a sunny day with a few scattered clouds. At the end of the sword's handle was a huge face. At first I thought it just another face in the clouds but as the wispy clouds blew across the sky, the face remained. I was with a group of friends walking in the countryside. Nine of us saw the face; two others refused to look up, they were scared.

The face stared down at us, it then looked across to a lake that was close by and then back at us. It had Middle Eastern features and it wore a pair of dark horned-rimmed glasses, which was very odd. After a while the face, which was the size of a block of apartments, started to morph into different faces. The original face with the horned-rimmed glasses became a skinhead type—your typical urban extremist. He then morphed into another male, who was a tribal ruler of some sort, then into a woman, who might have been his queen. She was similarly dressed. She was rather puzzling: she wore a skullcap as a head covering. To the right of her appeared another image and, over a period of six hours, more and more faces morphed into view, about fifty in all. Some looked Jewish. Some were urban skinheads. One was a Celtic-looking man on a throne. He had a staff in his hand; he looked like he enjoyed lording over people.

The spooky faces in the sky were alive; their heads and their eyes moved back and forth. It was hard to figure out what they were. The faces were not benevolent. They gazed down upon us with disdain just watching. It was one of the weirdest transdimensional experiences of my life. The experience seemed to be saying, "Hey, look up, there is influence above you that you have not seen before." But the influence wasn't just up in the sky; I realized it was also all around us. A couple of weeks after the sky people event, I saw the same faces, but very much smaller, in and around a good friend of mine. We were standing in her sitting room at nine in the morning chatting. The faces hung around her as clear as day. They were exactly the same faces we'd seen before. It was so odd.

Next, something utterly bizarre happened, which I mentioned before. There appeared on a blank wall of the sitting room a mysterious video presentation. The screen was about the size of a large TV and it jiggled about, up and down, left and right—it was slightly unstable at first. The film began in black and white, like a 1930s movie, and then played in brown sepia colors. Eventually, after a few minutes, it developed real color. The eventual color of the film was not the bright, almost gaudy colors of modern films we are used to; this video was lightly dusted with color. So the greens were not vibrant and there were almost no reds and yellows, though in one scene I remember lavender bushes, the violet flowers lightly colored.

How a video presentation appeared on the wall of a suburban London home without a projector or a monitor is completely beyond me. My friend and I (who I will call Sally as I am sure she would prefer not to be named), watched the video film that appeared mysteriously on the wall for 45 minutes. As the film was projected on the wall, it somehow tugged at our navels. That made us slightly nauseous. It reminded me of the author Carlos Castaneda, who mentioned in one of his books that your 'attention' tugs on your navel. The film was very tiring to watch; it took a lot of concentration to keep on watching it. I watched a film of a cat in a forest that could perform amazing tricks. It fought with other animals. From time to time, humans passed through the scene, morphing out of existence a few seconds later. Every few minutes the camera, if I can call it that, would run up a very tall pine tree. The POV (point of view) of the camera was just six inches or so away from the trunk of the trees. As it ran quickly up the truck, I remember feeling somewhat queasy. I don't have much of a head for heights. At the top of each tree, I heard the words in my mind, "Look at the stars. Look at the stars." The instructions were most insistent, "Look at the stars!"

As I looked up, I saw only blue sky and in the sky were the faces of the spooky sky people. They were everywhere. I tried to look at the stars but I couldn't see any. There were only faces up there. The camera's POV would then descend the tree and return once more to the cat's actions. Then a moment later up another pine tree it would go. I kept hearing, "Look at the stars." I couldn't see any stars, only sky people. Thirty-seven times in about 45 minutes, I went up a tree with the camera and down again. I couldn't understand it. It was a bit frustrating. It was also making me feel unwell. "Where are the stars?" I asked. I couldn't see them. I finally realized that was the point of the exercise. The film was saying you can't see the stars because the fascist oriented sky people control the sky. They are placed between you and the stars. The stars have something to do with the body of Christ. They represent our nostalgia for eternity. They represent God. When you sleep out under the stars, you get closer to God.

What was equally strange was that my friend Sally, who was watching the same section of living room wall, saw an entirely different video. She couldn't see my video and she didn't hear the words, "Look at the stars." In fact, she had no idea what I was watching and I in turn could not see her film. She saw a forty-five minute film about industrial workers, restriction and control, and NASA. Since that time in England, she has seen several more videos. I have only seen one more. It appeared on the wall of a hotel in New Orleans. It was short compared to the first one, a few minutes long at the most. There wasn't much action at all, just wild animals, giraffes, zebras, lions, and so on, walking slowly across a sunny plain that looked like Africa. The animals seemed very natural, content, and free.

I have since seen the sky people in other locations, but never as clearly as the first time I saw them on that country walk back in September 1999. The sky people are the trapped dead: ones who died with dark or elitist tendencies; people with no kindness or benevolence who died inside their hideous 'I'm so special,' mind-set.

I must take care to point out that the sky people are not only Jewish. And obviously, many modern Jewish folk are as liberal and as spiritual as anyone else. The bulk of wartime Jews were perhaps trapped, as I said, because they were seriously committed to fascist ideals and an elitist tribal vibe. But things change at an ordinary level, just as modern Germans or Italians are more liberal and spiritual than their fascist wartime ancestors, so too are individual Jews. People are evolving in spite of the control.

Hold the sky people idea and let us return to UFOs and disinformation. The whole of UFO research is littered with characters who are feeding us disinformation. Some of them are well meaning and are led along by phony 'inside' information that they repeat verbatim. Linda Moulton Howe, the UFO and crop researcher is one such person. She means well, even though she doesn't have a clue. Researchers and writers compete to be the one who is currently offering the hot inside information. It's natural that they would sometimes fall for a story that sounded genuine but was fed to them from a source of disinformation. Most researchers would agree that it is fair to say, after 50 years of UFO research, that none of them is any the wiser. It's all still conjecture and mystery. That is because it is deliberately planned that way. Stick a few facts in with a lot of bullshit, confirm nothing and contradict everything, and you'll control the situation forever.

The people in real power at the top do not want you to know what UFOs are all about. Because if you figure out the UFOs in the air, you'll eventually figure out how demonic 'the messengers of deception' are on the ground. Ding! Ding! Wakey-wakey. And you'll start to think about who is really running the show on the ground, pretending they are not running the show on the ground.

Because the UFOs rather undermine the regular military power-base, by having high-tech flying devices doing as they wish in our supposedly protected airspaces, it is not good for morale. The first reaction is always denial. The second reaction is usually disinformation: balloons, shooting stars, satellites reentering the Earth's atmosphere, blah, blah, which may explain some of what people see but it doesn't explain 90 percent of what's going on. The third reaction is propaganda—make anyone investigating the truth seem like a nutcase or an anarchist.

Some honest military men may know the real truth, but they are ordered to be silent by the top brass to protect the idea that our skies are invulnerable. Most UFOs, once they descend into the hotter parts of the color spectrum, can be picked up on radar. Tracking systems like NORAD just ignore them, as there is nothing they can do. Planes have been sent to intercept them, but the UFOs either hightail it out of there or the military planes are lost in action.

You can work everything out by moving in the opposite direction to the perceived spoon-fed wisdom. Officially, UFOs do not exist. Which tells you they must exist. Semi-officially they do exist but we are sold on the idea they are rare and benign: 'ET go home' and other syrupy explanations. The even less official position that some military personnel are quoted as saying in secret, is that UFOs do exist, that they are very rare, benign, solid craft from other planets or star systems, and isn't that interesting? They must be here to help us in some way. Colonel Corso's ludicrous 'technological gifts from outer space' story, for example. The opposite of this is, they are neither rare nor benign, they are not solid craft from another planet, and there is no evidence that they are helping in anyway whatsoever. Quite the reverse in fact.

It takes almost nothing to sustain a folklore myth for decades. Take Bob Lazar, a hero among UFO researchers. He says he worked at Area 51. He was formally employed at the Sandia Labs at Los Alamos, New Mexico, where he tells us he was bored with his lot in life. So he writes to the most famous physicist in the world, Edward Teller, asking for a new job. Brother Edward has bushy eyebrows and a very creepy vibe. He's known as the father of the hydrogen bomb. Ding! Teller replies to Lazar, a man he has never met, and suggests that Lazar transfer to a job at Area 51, which Teller duly arranges, or so the story goes. Excuse me, what's going on here? Do they think we are complete idiots? Obviously they do. Whatever next?

So Bob Lazar is working at Area 51, supposedly back-engineering propulsion technology from a UFO in the American Air Force's possession. "It is driven by an unheard of heavy element called element 115," says Bob. Element 115, according to Bob, can bend space and time to allow a UFO to be sucked into another star system in a flash. (May the force be with you Bob, that's the biggest load of drivel we've ever heard. Nice try.) Bob says there are a number of solid UFOs parked at Area 51, but that he did not work on these. After a while Bob gets bored with what to some would be the most interesting job in science, and quits his job. He now decides to spill the beans and jeopardize his life, as well as Teller's reputation. Lazar says the US Air Force has it own flying UFOs at Area 51, and anyone who wants to verify this can go along to the black mailbox on the extraterrestrial highway in Nevada. There, on certain evenings of the week, at a predetermined time (it's not polite to keep the press waiting), they can videotape the American UFOs being tested, flying about in the distance over a nearby ridge.

Jeez, that's good news.

Japanese TV shows up along with other researchers and the solid-UFO-in-America-procession plops gently into folklore as intended. Imagine, if the US really did have solid flying UFOs, would they put them up on show regularly at 8:30pm every Wednesday evening for people to photograph? Have they done that with any other of their military projects? I don't think so. Ding! Ding! Wake up. What's going on here? Disinformation.

Now Brother Bob, after he left Area 51 and spilt the beans on what was supposedly the greatest secret ever, continued to live in the area, making regular appearances on TV. What did the military do? Nothing. Was he arrested? No, he wasn't. He claimed he was shot at but even that doesn't ring true. Certainly the security forces didn't shoot at him because they don't miss. Anyway, suicides, single-engine planes that crash, and overdoses of undetectable drugs (insulin), which look like heart attacks to a coroner, are the disposable diaper of choice. You have to grant the military a bit of respect. Their business is killing people; pinging a few pot shots off a dissident's car on the freeway is not a military way of operating. No. I think Lazar's claim about being shot at is part of his elaborate story. Or, maybe someone totally unrelated to Area 51, like an ex maybe, got pissed off with Brother Bob.

A few junior workers at Area 51 get on TV and back the flying UFO story, saying they have seen little buggy-eyed Greys working side-by-side with American servicemen at the Nevada facility. These workers didn't get into trouble either. It seems the American military doesn't care who is spilling the beans on their cherished secrets, and anyone can get away with it unpunished. Another ding, ding? You'd certainly have to think so, wouldn't you? Definitely ding, ding material I'd say.

Just for fun, what is the opposite of Bob Lazar's story? I'd hazard a guess that if the Americans did have their own UFOs, they would not be testing them in front of Japanese TV at a predetermined time and place. Second, I'd guess that Bob and the other whistleblowers would be dead or in the slammer. Third, if there is an element 115, we know it would be very unstable—it would decay within less than a split second. How an American-made UFO in Nevada uses 115 to stay aloft long enough for the TV crews to get a good look at it is one for the cuckoo that flew over the nest.

Whatever Bob is saying, someone somewhere has authorized it. Maybe he never worked at Area 51, or he did work there but not in the capacity he describes. The game is to lace a bit of truth in amongst the BS. But whatever way you look at Lazar's story, it doesn't hold water. Though, surprise, surprise, it is repeated as gospel truth on every TV show that ever gets made about UFOs.

Roswell, Blue Book, Majestic12, Lazar, and much of the myth-building all points the same way. The only guy, Vallee, that pointed the other way, has quit the UFO scene. The 'constructed' folklore says that UFOs are from outer space. There is no evidence to support that premise. We are also sold the idea that they are solid nuts-and-bolts craft.

After 50 years there is no credible evidence of that, though there is a little circumstantial evidence, if you believe the Lonnie Zamora story. (He was a police officer, which should add credibility.) That's not to say Zamora was lying, only to say that he was chosen to see the on-the-ground UFO, and then his story could enter folklore as truth.

The myth goes on to say, as I've mentioned, that the Americans have their own UFOs, and that UFOs are generally benign. Of course, the Americans having their own UFOs, if the real UFOs are not benign, is very handy. Then the Yanks can send up theirs to chase the bad guys away and keep the 'home of the brave' free from any extraterrestrial intrusions. Do you see how this game is played? There are 115 levels of bullshit. If you pick up almost any UFO book you'll see the Lazar story in it along with other UFO folklore classics, and you will never see anyone ask, "What kind of fool am I?" People suck on these stories almost without question. I came to wonder who's writing the books and why?

But you have to constantly return to the idea that the UFOs and the people in control on the ground are one and the same. Neither wants you to know what is happening. It took me a long time to accept the idea of the sky people, especially as what I saw was simply an allegorical way to describe their control. The sky people are inches from you in your etheric and they are seriously in left field, i.e. satanic. What they have in common with the fat controllers is their rapacious and loveless nature toward humanity and a desire to control, which is their desire for immortality. I kept saying, "No. No. I can't accept it." But the more I ran from the idea, the more it chased me.

I would look up and I'd see them. Maybe you don't see them yet because your eyes are closed to it. But once you aren't scared to look up, you'll see them. It's hard to see them on very bright days, just as the etheric is hard to see under bright light. It's easier to see the sky people on cloudy days. Of course, the sky people are really inches away from your left or right ear; the faces in the sky are just an extension of an etheric phenomenon that's all around you. When you walk, it walks with you. It's thinking for you a lot of the time. It's the neo-Nazi cult of 'the Chosen One,' which fell from heaven into the intoxication of material power, money, glitz, and the false gods of the ego—the gods of immortality.

The neo-Nazis have successfully put themselves between God and the people. They are the devilish etheric entities, the new camp commandants, the tyrannical police officer, the violent father, the manipulative mother, the crooks, and the parasites that feed off humanity. It's a numeric thing, the more that died, the more power generated in the nearby etheric. They can inhibit the flow of light, the light of the Great Goodness (God) that trickles through. But more than anything else, they manage to cut off the escape routes people have been trying to find to leave the earth plane at death. It is way more difficult nowadays than it was 50 years ago.

The number of the dead in the nearby etheric is impossible to work out. The UFOs in the air were calculated with the aid of helpers at 60,000, a figure said to be inaccurately low by mid-1999. I have no way of knowing if that figure is accurate or not. Also, I don't know if that includes the UFOs that are in the earth and under the sea. Furthermore, it's impossible to say how many transdimensionals there are (Greys, Reptilians, Nordics, Nefilim, Watchers, and so on). I've only seen one Reptilian and maybe twenty Greys, but I have never seen more than three Greys together at any one time. They all look the same, so I can't tell if I am looking at different Greys or the same few over and over.

When I first came to see the terror of their influence, I lay down and quit. I couldn't figure out how on earth we might manage. The transdimensionals are feeding thoughts to the fat controllers, who are everywhere. And it's a part of most people's dream to become a fat controller; it feels safe to them. If you give 'em even an insignificant uniform, say a traffic warden uniform, they become a little Nazi as fast as they feasibly can.

I wondered how we would fight back, we seem so powerless. We have very few resources, no voice, no political power, very little money, and if we do fight back, we have to face the thought police who are brilliant at bending perception so the tyrants seem the victims and vice versa. The thought police control the voice on the ground, and anyone who objects will have to handle the objection at ground level as well as the terror of the transdimensional administration above. They are not keen on anyone who blows the whistle on the domination scam. At first glace they hold all the power, they are the sharks, and they are mean and dangerous, especially the transdimensionals. I've seen them come through the walls. They can scan your mind. They can paralyze you by freezing the air around you so you become immobile. They seem to have us by the short and curlies. But they don't have all the cards, for if the truth be known they are terrified of us. They are particularly scared of anyone who can countermand their power.

Normally, they go after humans who succumb to fear, and in that situation the transdimensionals have all the power. But if they bump into someone who knows what he or she is doing, someone who's fearless, who doesn't give a shit, then the shoe is on the other foot. In a way, we are stronger than them, but we have to come to believe it. The only way to believe it is to suffer the fear and go beyond it. I started running around the house at 3am with my mates, samurai swords drawn, chasing the Greys up the hallway. Were the Greys scared? I don't know, but they sure fucked off quick. Suddenly, here's this guy in the hallway who doesn't give a shit and is about to take ya fucking head off. You see, the secret is don't flinch. But it takes a while to get to that, as you can't 'not flinch' until you go through the terror training. That's the way to become brave and strong.

Etheric perception? We've got that. Mindscan? No big deal, we can do that. Walk through walls? Been there, done that, got the T-shirt. The only thing that is missing is solidifying the air to immobilize people. That one is tricky. We can't work it out just yet. It will come, we'll figure it out—we've got helpers, finally. We reached up for them and once we became fearless, they were able to reach down to us. Before that, all they could do was feel sorry for us. There was nothing else they could do; we were too feeble and too scared. You can't defend a person when they are scared. But once the helpers could reach down, it changed our lives, big time. We realized we're faster than the transdimensionals and we have the nostalgia as well. After 18 months head to head with the Greys, we chased them out of the house and they never came back.

But the danger isn't them so much—the Greys and the UFOs are rinky-dink bullshit—the real danger is the conscious and unconscious mind of man, which is everywhere: it's a sea of nastiness and pain. It causes me an enormous amount of despair. When I said there were only five percent or so who could get out, I was referring to today's conditions; within a decade it will dwindle to even less. The doors are closing. We'll be down to .00002 percent per million. So 5,000 in America, 1,000 in

Britain, 340 in Australia, 80 in New Zealand—it's hardly
any. With surveillance technology, the sharks will be able
to watch your every move. It is exactly the world they
want, one where no one can escape. Everyone will have
to bow down and worship the shark. We will all be asked
to accept the false gods invented by the fat controllers,
the money printers, the lenders, insurance, hype, media,
glitz, power, and glamour; each will have to worship at
the altar of Babylon, or walk away. To walk is
unbelievably lonely. But there are Gladiators out there,
and they are full of love and will greet you once you
arrive. Sadly, they can't come back for you, you have to
walk out of the prison and join them.

Imagine looking at all that stuff on TV and saying,
"Bullshit, I don't need a Porsche, it's too elitist. Those gaudy
Versace clothes? I don't need them either. And the extended
multiple orgasm for $49.95? No thanks. One orgasm at
a time is just fine. If they come chain ganged, all well and
good, but I ain't paying extra for them. And by the way,
I don't need the panty-pads with the little wings on 'em
either. I am me. I am free. What do I need all this bullshit
for?" It is very hard to look in the eye of authority and
the overall programming of the fat controllers and say,
"You are an illusion. Do me a favor, fuck off."

It's hard. People don't normally have that kind of
courage. They have never seen the open country; they are
raised as drones. Anyway, they often have deep within a

powerful subconscious alignment with the very ideals of control and drone land. They pretend to be freedom loving and kind, but in reality they like to control and inflict pain on others, it helps them to feel important and safe. Every second of every day another person, somewhere, sells their soul forever. They become another camp guard in return for the illusion of a phony immortality, specialness, status, and the security offered by the company of the other fat controllers.

In the end, the only escape is perception and that develops gradually within you. Eventually it starts to talk to you and it tells you which way to go. It says don't fall for materialism, consumerism, fascism, the UN, EU, CNN, ABC, BBC, UPI, and all that BS, walk the other way. Comprehend that it's a lie. Look at the forces of control, they are paper tigers, they are utterly powerless if you refuse to give them your power. The fall of communist Russia is a good example.

Do you have to bother to fight these petty tyrants? No, it's not worth it, and anyway it's not allowed. They will destroy themselves. We can only love them for their pathetic weakness. How will you challenge the system? There is no point. In challenging it you have to wrestle with it. They will always have the upper hand: they own the media, they print the money, they guard every exit—you can't beat them. They are the field and the field won't let you get through to the public if your message contradicts it. You will get booked for a TV show and it will be cancelled. You will give an interview and it will never appear in print. You will get asked to do a radio show and at the last minute they will tell you something has happened and you are not on. You'll write a book and it won't get published. You will book a lecture hall and someone will try to cancel the hall behind your back. Author David Icke told me he gets this a lot. Members of the B'nai B'rith call and try to get David's gigs cancelled by threatening the hall owners. B'nai B'rith, and the so-called Defamation League, is a form of Jewish thought police. Its function is to produce propaganda and eliminate any contradictory opinion. They don't like Icke because he talks about the Jewish families that control the world. Of course, Icke is not insulting or defaming anyone. It's just that the thought police don't like it, and they are linked to the Israeli secret service, a fact that is common knowledge. So it would be like the CIA threatening the owner of a hall, getting them to cancel your appearance, because you wrote a book that said you thought America was becoming a police state.

   Conspiracy theorists will say it's a plot by the Jews; others will say it's the Illuminati or the Freemasons, and some believe big business and the political systems have conspired to exercise supreme control over our citizens. Of course, they have. Others say Eisenhower sold out to the UFOs in a deal brokered at Edwards Air Force base in the early '50s. Endless books tell of world control by an inner secret government, the extensions of which are the Council of Foreign Affairs, the Trilateral Commission, the Bohemian Grove, the Bildebergers, and so on. In a way, the conspiracy theorists are right and in a way they are completely wrong.

The problem is, none of these conspiracies have ever really been proven. The idea that the big families run the world is obvious; but the conspiratorial nature of it all has not been proven in my view. I don't think there is a conspiracy, as most of the people involved aren't clever enough, and the power elite fights like crazy amongst itself anyway. A shark will eat another shark before it will eat us little minnows—its ego feels good when it eats important sharks. Remember, these types are used to eating little people all day long; when a real big fish comes along they must salivate profusely.

No. I don't think there is a conspiracy. The Sphere and the field itself is the conspiracy. It will not allow anyone to challenge its overall power. The field is connected to everyone. So the man at the radio station who cancels your show is acting on the prompting of the field, which finds congruence in his need to control and eliminate any opposition. It's unlikely that he knows the guys at the B'nai B'rith who are trying to get David Icke's appearance cancelled in Toronto. They in turn are not connected to the manipulators in the financial markets who act to sustain themselves just as the shark acts to sustain itself by eating seals in the inlet. The conspiracy is that the field will never allow you to step beyond its desire for itself, which is the control mechanism. To go beyond it you have to be brave and very sure of yourself.

It's not as if the field has just a few thousand on its side, it has hundreds of millions on its side. Everyone you look at is a potential agent of the Sphere and its field. There is no way of telling who are trapped and who are not. Suffice to say, there is no field of human endeavor that is not under the control of the Luciferian/Ahrimanic forces.

In addition to that there is the brainwashing and programming in schools, universities, magazines, and papers. And people's ideas, endlessly telling you that you are powerless, that you should subjugate yourself to the greater good. Endlessly telling you that the thieves are honest and lies are truth. Who decides on the greater good? The fat controllers do of course. How many guesses do you need?

YOU CAN NEVER ESCAPE THE FIELD
UNTIL YOU CAN LET GO AND WALK AWAY FROM
THE PROGRAMMING. IT'S LONELY TO WALK
BUT IT'S WORSE TO STICK AROUND.

The world religions stand between you and God in an attempt to control spirituality. The media stands between you and truth. The military stands between you and peace. The bureaucracy stands between you and freedom. The police force stands between you and liberty. The politicians stand between you and the law (and invent systems of control to enrich themselves). The drug companies stand between you and health. It's all a control trip, the makings of a living hell.

But they cannot win against the individual, because the fat controllers are drones. Like the Greys that act in unison, two, three, or four at a time; they have no mind of their own. Like drones, they have a common, shared mind-set, and no originality that comes from an independent spirit and independent personal journey. They are drones captured by the Sphere. They live in the ghettos of the mind and they follow a pre-programmed set of instructions. It's part of humanity's desire for self-importance to follow a pre-programmed set of instructions.

Each follows the spoon-fed bullshit for 67 years, then keels over and is stuck in the ground side-by-side with the other drones. Why is it called a graveyard? Because death is seriously grave to some and you only get a yard to lie in.

Once you develop your individuality and once you are self sufficient, then you are no longer scared of the sharks and they cannot get you. There is, of course, an uncomfortable period when you leave the lagoon and have to swim blind through the sharks believing only in yourself. I didn't find it easy; there is a lot of terror, insecurity, sadness, hopelessness, grief, abandonment, and, sometimes, the elation of knowing you are heading out to sea, and because you haven't been eaten so far, the chances are you won't be eaten later on. It's difficult but it is not impossible.

What has driven me through the terror all these years is the idea that one day I'll get beyond the sharks. If one person manages to swim past them, then two or three others can follow, then four will get away, then forty will follow, and because of them 100,000 humans can flee. In the end, the sharks are stuffed. People can now escape and one of them could be you.

Yᴏᴜ ᴄᴀɴ ɴᴇᴠᴇʀ

ɢᴇᴛ ᴘᴀꜱᴛ ᴛʜᴇ ꜰɪᴇʟᴅ

ᴡʜɪʟᴇ ʏᴏᴜ

ᴀʀᴇ ꜱᴛɪʟʟ

ꜱᴄᴀʀᴇᴅ ᴏꜰ

ᴛʜᴇ ꜰᴀᴛ ᴄᴏɴᴛʀᴏʟʟᴇʀꜱ.

You can't move beyond the field until you see yourself bigger than the field, larger than life. This is not an egotistical, grandiose routine, it's just knowing that all the BS is maya—the grand illusion. It's pathetic, it has no power. The sharks are powerless against a seal or fish that has real individuality, a real spirituality, a real nostalgia for God.

It's not as if the little fish or seal can eat the shark; it can only swim past it. But in swimming past the shark you are fatally wounded by it. Yet the terrifying shark is in fact like a blow-up doll, similar to the ones at the porno shop. Once you understand that, you have understood the one great lesson in life.

For in the end, given the dual nature of our psychology, the Nazi's presence simply reflects people's fear. The nearby etheric transdimensionals and the trapped dead reflect the inner Nazi, the elitist within both you and me. The sharks and control trippers are part of humanity's darkness, and if they bother you, then, in part, you are attacking yourself. The moneylenders and the shysters that feed off little people are just an outer reflection of the meanness inside us that demands its pound of flesh, that demands vengeance for alleged crimes against us. That is why the little fish can't eat the shark, for in a way the shark is a part of the little fish. In most people, the 'inner shark' is not resolved and it causes trouble and traps them in a satanic noose. You can't move beyond the shark by fighting it. As said, you can only move beyond it by being silently bigger than it. You have to let go. If you don't let go, your soul will be trapped. The dorks will suffocate you within a psychological and spiritual death, which you will then see reflected in the utter meaninglessness of your daily life.

You have to let go of the need to control to escape the field. Every time you partake in a control trip, you pancake face down onto the field. To let go is scary. But after a while, I found not letting go was even scarier. Training one's mind to let go of the need to know takes time, but in the end it was so simple to just walk away and not think and not resist.

Yᴏᴜ ᴄᴀɴ ɴᴇᴠᴇʀ ɢᴇᴛ ᴏᴜᴛ
ᴏғ ᴛʜᴇ ғɪᴇʟᴅ
ᴜɴᴛɪʟ ʏᴏᴜ ᴅʀᴏᴘ ʏᴏᴜʀ ɴᴇᴇᴅ
ᴛᴏ ᴄᴏɴᴛʀᴏʟ.

12

ABDUCTIONS,
CROP CIRCLES,
CATTLE MUTILATIONS,
AND SO ON

Abductions are real, though not everyone's abduction is real. Some people must be lying to seek attention, or they are genuine but in error. By and large though, abductions are real and common.

I used to wonder if abductions were in the etheric, like an involuntary out-of-body experience, or were they an actual physical abduction where the body was transported elsewhere? I once saw an etheric gizmo, the size of a teacup, hover in my bedroom. It was a machine that probed my knee while I was awake lying on the bed. I whacked it hard with the back of my hand.

Anyway, I stayed with the etheric out-of-body version of abductions for a while. But then I began to wonder if this human body was even solid. Do you seriously imagine your body to be real and solid, I'd ask myself. I came to see it as not solid. Nothing is solid in its alternative state. There is no solid. So I finally rested with the idea that the Greys can convert your body into its less than solid state, which is how they can get you out of the room. Interestingly, they have to go through a window. They can't get you out through a wall, so maybe there are varying states of non-solid. Obviously, a window is a lot less solid than a wall— there's less resistance.

Are the Greys studying humans for some reason? I think not. They have been here a long time; there is nothing much else to find out. Are they breeding a new race? A crossbreed? Possibly, but I very much doubt it—sounds fishy to me. I think their main reason for abduction is to generate fear, and to keep selling the idea of technologically superior beings from another planet. Beings that one ought to bow down to and give away one's power to. As said, once an abductee is no longer scared, the abductions stop. So fear is a factor in abductions.

There was a conference held at the Massachusetts Institute of Technology (MIT), one of the most prestigious institutions of higher learning in the world. It was a conference on alien abduction, and a book was written on the findings of the conference. The conclusion of this book was that abductions are probably real and ain't it spooky? Who are these superior beings and what do their breeding programs mean, were a couple of the questions asked at the conference.

Excuse me! Ding! Ding! What's going on here? The most prestigious institute in the world, hosting a space cadets conference on UFOs and alien abductions? Surely MIT would be laughed out of the academic world. Why would they risk the ridicule that might follow? Because it would seem, someone, somewhere, wants the abduction story to become ever more real and scary. MIT must have been persuaded to hold the conference by someone in authority, as alien abductions are not on the usual curriculum. Having the abduction conference at MIT gave it credibility; it gave it the seal of approval from the authorities so to speak. Someone wants the story out there, scaring people stiff.

It's okay to be terrified of alien abductions; I was at first until I worked them out. The defense is to first realize that they have no more power than you potentially have. And next, you have to love them. It cannot be a false, mental type of love: "Oh, I love you so much," puke, puke. You've got to mean it. It's as if the power rises from the root chakra to your heart and you then project it

forward as a deep resounding etheric love, one the Greys can't resist. Other defenses work to some extent, but unfortunately the Greys can tamper with anything electrical. They don't like video cameras, and a permanent CCTV puts them off but is not foolproof. An infrared lamp that gives off violet light spooks 'em, and putting fields of electricity around your bed works: use copper wire and a battery. But that doesn't work for long, as the nearer you get to electricity the more likely it is to mutate your cells. Subatomic particles given off by electricity act as a knife and can cut a human cell in two. There is a definite link between leukemia and other cancers, and strong or nearby electrical fields. The Greys don't like strong light. Mostly they operate at night between 3 and 4am. While UFOs usually fly between 9 and 10pm. Tick-tock! Even the transdimensionals have working hours. Spooky.

Some crop circles are real and they are manifestations of the Goddess talking to us about the fractal nature of the universe. Other circles are misinformation by transdimensionals seeking attention. It's part of the ploy to sell people the idea of higher beings from outer space. The Daily Mail in the UK, a true blue propaganda outfit, writes ludicrous stories during the crop circle season. It says that the circles are made by blokes with planks. It creates deliberate falsehoods, saying that the field is sown with wheat when it is barley, or it incorrectly describes the location of the field, and so forth. The Daily Mail claims two guys can make a 300 yard wide crop circle with two planks, in the dark, in three hours with absolute mathematical precision without being seen. Ding! Plonk! Pass the plank. The idea of course is to strengthen the beliefs of the faithful, much in the same way as the alleged crash at Roswell has strengthened the idea of solid UFOs. The secondary ploy is to confuse and scare people.

There is a theory that crop circles are formed by earth spirits who want to help people achieve a higher consciousness. I don't accept that theory—too dippy. Anyway, they are part of a different evolution, one that has nothing to do with humans and our evolution. Crop circles are mostly transdimensional UFO-type activity—spooky activity.

Cattle mutilations are real. They seem to occur mostly in northern New Mexico and southern Colorado. The military has been linked to cattle mutilations, but I think it's the transdimensionals. They may be studying cows, but I doubt it. There isn't much to a cow that they couldn't learn real quick if they wanted to. They are mutilating cattle for the same reason they do everything else: to create mystery and fear. It also strengthens the illusion of their phony genetic research. The bullshit of the Grey's genetic research only started after we discovered DNA; before that there was no mention of genetics. I also don't buy the idea that the cow is food for them. Unless they use the blood in some way I don't know about. An etheric being would not be able to digest meat. Greys don't seem to have a digestive system. The food theory is out. I feel sorry for the cows. Then again, humans don't treat cows real well either.

What else? Men in black: apparitions dressed in kit from the late '40s and '50s? Just another shape shift.

Reptilians? Now they exist for real and are entities that look like reptilians and are highly intelligent and very loving. The Reptilians associated with the UFOs seem to be of another mind-set. I have only ever seen one and it was scary, mean, and cruel. Others have seen them though. However, the idea that Reptilians take on human form and become the British royalty is unproven in my view. I don't think they really need to adopt human form as they can enter the mind of anyone who will accept their message, as can you.

Mindscan is the process described by abductees whereby the Greys or the Nordics stare into the abductees' eyes close up and read or download the contents of their mind. This sounds true, though I have never seen it done myself. But it's easily doable and nothing special: simply more posturing by the Greys in my view. It's all posturing in my view, on the ground and above it.

13

More Disinformation

We've talked about social, political, and commercial disinformation—it's everywhere. What about other disinformation? The churches are the custodians of much of it. They often attempt to bind you emotionally while they milk you. The word religion comes from the Latin word to bind. The churches also try to place their theory or dogma between you and God. That is a crime against humanity—Dawn Trader country. You are not allowed to promise redemption to anyone, and it's especially evil if you have to join something or follow something to get it. Over the long-term, these modern churches won't last, and the Catholic Church is particularly vulnerable to collapse, as its political corruption is rife. Furthermore, the priests' reputation has been tarnished as the sexual abuse scandals have surfaced. The main problem the Church faces is that people are fleeing from it in droves, so money will eventually become an issue. But the worse problem is, young men now won't enter the priesthood. The Church could revive its fortunes if it allowed women to take Holy Orders, but I wonder if it has the courage to reform in this way.

The New Age is riddled with the false prophets I mentioned before. As are the Spiritualist churches, which are susceptible to influence from nearby entities posing as someone's granny. Channeling is also prone to the same crossover interference. Reiki is wide open and it's selling bogus technology. It's based on a lie, an insidious con. (I'll explain later.) Some of the meditation gurus play the same game hoping to indoctrinate you. "Here's ya mantra, go off and meditate." Spew, brother, spew. Yoga, over a long time, will debilitate you and rob you of your energy—it may even kill you eventually. Yoga is very spooky.

Meditation is easy: buy a metronome tape and learn to sit in trance. You don't need anyone to help you with it, you can be self-directed. Vipassana, forget it. It's tough to comprehend that most of the stuff you think is so great is disinformation and a control trip at worse, or at best, something you don't need. Acupuncture works and it's okay, as is almost all bodywork. As long as the practitioner is not manipulating you, no problem. Go for it if, it helps you. Martial arts is not a problem, it helps your confidence, strength, and fitness. And as long as your teacher offers a clearly marked exit sign, it's no worry at all.

Kirlian photography is pure rubbish: it's damp and heat they photograph. Aura photos? A con. If you watch carefully you'll see the photographer twiddling the knobs to alter the color of the lens from customer to customer. There's a guy I know who has made a million bucks from knob twiddling. He rests warm in his bed for now. Feng Shui? The sensitive picks up on the flow of energy in your home or office and hopefully gives you some accurate advice. There is no harm in it in my view. It's next to worthless; you can work it out for yourself. But if you fancy the idea, why not?

Health food, vitamins, potions, aromatherapy, and so on? If you like them and they help you, great. Bach flower remedies are a placebo. They will work if you believe in them and don't think too much. Don't read the brochure. It's from Munchkin Land.

"Mind Control to Major Tom" where the fuck's the New Age gone? Some of it has hit the straight and narrow, and the dodgy bit that traps and misinforms is falling by the wayside. It's easy to work out. If someone really loves you, or if a method is really useful, it will feel right and your teacher will help set you free. There won't be any power trip or control. You'll pay for your instruction and the teacher will leave and there's nothing more to it. Unless, of course, you want to repeat what he or she taught. But teachings that jump from the beginner's course, to the intermediate course, to the advanced accredited master's course, are bullshit. These courses are designed by agents of the Sphere. What they teach must be suspect as they are designed as entrapment—be careful.

Magic is a trap. It's a power trip. Astrology is harmless. So are the other divination tools: tarot, tea leaves, I Ching, and so on. Remember this: if a spiritual or religious practice gives you calm and serenity, then it's fine for a short time. But once it gets into elitism, or immortality, it is selling you a trap here on Earth and a further trap down the line in the spirit world. If you have been programmed to believe in this stuff like I was, it will take you a while to see the Sphere-like nature of it all. It took me about six months of resistance before I quit and agreed with the Gladiators. There is no rush; but in the end you won't need spiritual practices, as God is not 'spiritual' in our sense of the word. And the practices are a trap.

It's hard at first to comprehend that you can make it on your own. That you have to make it on your own if you want to escape. It's all in you. You have the power, no one else. You are sacred and special, not more important than others, but special in the sense that you are a child of creation. You can teach yourself. I did. I didn't get what I know from books. I met a few wizards on the way who helped me out with some particular expertise, but 90 percent of the time I taught myself. I insisted on wisdom and as it entered my perception, I proceeded very carefully, double-checking facts all the way. You can do the same. Then again you might insist that the Gladiator's help you. There are inner ones as well as human ones that you might meet—demand that someone, somewhere, show you the truth. Fight for it. Insist on it. Pray for it. Go to silence and you will start to find it and eventually, when you are ready, it finds you.

I was shocked when I realized things were often placed backwards. We are sold on the idea that daytime is safe and good and that nighttime is unsafe and not so good—quite the reverse. Nighttime is the only time you can communicate unhindered. It's very safe compared to the day time for most of the nearby human minds are asleep, leaving you unhindered. Sunlight destroys melatonin, which is vital for ESP. Why are sunny holidays so cheap? For perception you need moisture in the air and darkness. Here's a cheap holiday in a dry sunny place, try that. Why are surfers who spend all day in the sun usually none too bright. Why is melatonin banned in sunny Australia? Ding! By the way, fear often arises from dehydration. When your body is dry, it destroys your perception and makes you more scared. Most people don't drink enough clean water. If you drink four liters (about eight pints) of water and take a couple of lecithin tablets each day, you can re-hydrate your body over a period of several weeks. You will, however, notice your fear lessen within a few days. I've been told you need the lecithin oil to carry the water to the cells.

Here's another control trip: it's one that says if you follow the religious and institutional rules you will be saved, you will be considered good, and you will go to heaven, and if you don't follow the rules, you will perish. It's quite the reverse. If you follow the rules, you'll wind up with the rule makers in the nearby etheric, trapped. Whoops! That doesn't mean you should embrace evil, it just means their rules will direct you to their spirit worlds, devilish ones and celestial ones. Same trap.

We are told that cause creates the effect. We call it the law of cause and effect. But it's quite the reverse: it's the effect returning from the future that establishes the cause. Get ya brain around that one! Which way is time running? Forward in the free will version and backward in the divine plan; but, anyway, one level up and there is no time. Stay away from worrying about time; it will drive you crackers.

We were told we descended from apes. In school, there was probably a chart that showed apes rising to become Neanderthals who eventually become the squeaky clean nude white man, his wife, and kid standing hand-in-hand. Modern man is not related to the Neanderthals. Sorry. Now what? And because humans are now taller and brighter than we previously imagined them to be, we are convinced we are evolving. We are not evolving, if you take a long enough timeline we are devolving and becoming colder. Taller and brighter and living longer is not the criteria for evolution, just our criteria. Anyway, there are others here that are taller and brighter than we will ever be. Meanwhile, we are also devolving spiritually, for the more advanced technologically we become, the more hell we create. Oh, dear!

Why is hell wrongly sold as hot, with no mention of the temperature of heaven? Hell is described as hot to scare you, and to keep you in the fold. If you miss church, you have sinned. And if you die in sin, you go to a fiery hell. Rubbish. Heaven is warm. The Grail is warm. The Goddess is warm. Hell is like the transdimensionals, merciless and cold, and they often smell of sulfur, like rotten eggs.

Talking of rotten eggs, you know those healers who tell you that they can heal you with the energy of their hands, and that they are a pure conduit for God's light, blah, blah—the squeaky clean, chosen ones. Well, that's pure crap. Humans are inside out. The light of infinity (God) is experienced, almost as if in slow motion, as an explosion from within. Yet, the healer feels the etheric warmth of his or her kundalini passing through their hands to the patient's body, and it suits their importance to claim that it is God's light. It's not. It's sex. It is moved from the healer's sex chakra via their hands to the patient through desire for recognition. Be clear, the light of God flows the other way, from within the body toward the surface of your skin. Ding! Ding! If you truly want to heal people, you take the affected part of their body and see it hovering in eternity. Then, just pointing at it, you explode the love of God through it and around it, and that love of God explodes like the Big Bang, passing from infinity through the atoms and molecules of the cells and eventually outwards through the skin. The other way is just an ego wank and doesn't work. By taking the patient to infinity you take them to their non-solid state where they return to God and remember that their body is perfect.

Seek and ye shall find. The more you travel out to find what you are looking for, the less you will find it. You may have already experienced that. Sit still and in silence and 'ye will find.' Seek not. The Kingdom of God is all around you. You don't have to go anywhere.

"Give and thou shall receive," the churches say, hoping for your money. The fact is, when you give money from your emotions or your mind, it doesn't make a blind bit of difference. It's only when you give your money or love unconditionally that you receive. All the rest is a waste of time. It's agenda oriented, expressing the will of the ego. Here's my donation, where's my pay? It doesn't work. It's odd that people have not noticed that.

Death is scary and birth is glorious, they say. Excuse me! Death is heaven and easy, a liberation. Birth I'd imagine, though I can't quite remember, must be scary and very stressful. Imagine coming from some place warm and nurturing, where you have the comfort of your mother's heartbeat, into bright lights and noise and someone whacking you on the bum.

It's all sold to you backwards to make sure you never figure it out. Never forget that the Sphere is very clever.

14

The End Run

This is Chapter 7 continued.

Let's talk about escape from the Sphere. The first step is to bag tick-tock and look for another way of making ends meet. That may require you to simplify your life and reduce your financial needs. Next, get rid of anyone in your life who's a control-tripper—out! Leave anywhere or any situation where you are not free to negotiate your liberation, go freelance maybe.

Throw out the papers and the TV. If you can't bring yourself to chuck out the TV, use it just for watching videos. When you watch videos, be careful. They are often made by agents of the Sphere—take it all with a grain of salt. They are often selling low-grade fear, or outright horror and violence—etheric food. They also sell conformity. Conformity presses on you, forcing you to stay where you are. Plan an escape from conformity. Remember, even hippy style non-conformity is a type of conformity.

If you smoke pot you've got no chance. It makes you docile and it tears your etheric; but its worse feature is that it gradually poisons your brain making you paranoid. You'll lack the courage and impetus to run. Cocaine increases your chance of a heart attack by 27 times and kills you eventually, and heroin also makes you docile. Speed? Forget it. Special K? Forget it. DMT—try it twice. LSD is worthless, mind diarrhea, nothing more. Magic mushrooms can take you to other worlds, but they can make you paranoid if you take too big a dose. Okay in small quantities. Peyote? Good for throwing up. I'm not sure it has any other uses. Ecstasy opens your heart and it helps you to feel—might be detrimental long-term if you take a lot of it. The ecstasy 'death' stories in the media are propaganda. No one has ever died of it, unless they had something wrong with them in the first place, or they died of dehydration. More people die of a lack of love. Seven hundred and fifty thousand tabs of ecstasy go down every weekend in the UK, very few people die. If you gave 750,000 people lemonade, one or two might die by chance, if their heart conked out just after the drink. I think opening your heart is a good thing;

though I can't say if ecstasy is the way to go—you choose. (I'm not here to wag the finger at personal habits, that's the Sphere's game.) Alcohol is okay in small doses, a couple of drinks a day; anything over that and it becomes a control mechanism. I had to give it up to get where I wanted to go. That was a sad day. Smokes? They're okay—you choose. Gambling? Out. Pornography? Out.

Now what? Ready to run, let's go!

In the physical body, you will die and wind up in the nearby etheric with the odious sky people, or you'll drift to what people call spirit worlds. I've been to some of these worlds. Some are grim in their blandness and others are quite cheery and look like scenes from a sunny holiday in Tuscany. All these worlds are still in the Sphere. It's a trap. The celestial worlds bathed in celestial light are also a trap. I didn't see that til later. They are elevated spirit worlds, but they are part of the Sphere.

Now look at your hand. Is it solid, can you see it? If you can, you're still here in the Sphere. If you can see your bones, you are on the cusp. To get out, you dematerialize. Don't be daunted, morphing out of this 3-D reality is a lot easier than you think. When it starts, the morph first appears as colored geometric lines—as grids and colored fractal patterns on your forehead. Then they spread over your entire body. They are indescribably beautiful. There are no words adequate enough. It's God in geometric Technicolor. When the morph appears, on your forehead say, another person can put their finger right into your skull. It's very funny and yet rather weird to watch. It doesn't hurt. The body is not solid at that point. When they pull their finger out, it is strangely elongated, stretching to about double its normal length. The finger becomes wet (soapy) and pointed. This suggests to me that the non-solid world beyond the morph may be traveling faster than light. Things approaching the speed of light become shorter in length, and the modern hypothesis is, when traveling faster than light, things become longer. This is correct in my view.

Associated with the phenomena is a fluttering sensation that may continue for several months and even years. And the phenomena that I call helicopter blood, where one gets the impression that one's cells are spinning, faster and faster. This is often accompanied with a feeling of extreme heaviness. One becomes so heavy that one can do nothing but lie down. This suggests to me that perhaps the atoms of your cells are jiggling at something close to the speed of light, for scientists know that if you approach the speed of light you would find yourself getting heavier and heavier. Then after a few days you seem to reach a zero point where you break through to the other side and you begin to feel your normal weight, or even lighter. The odd part of this is, it seems that at that point one's cells are going backwards in time, for you experience a prickling sensation and you can watch your skin rejuvenate in front of your eyes. Marks like liver spots on your hand disappear in a matter of hours and your skin becomes glowing and soft, as it might have been when you were a young person. I've got a feeling that real immortality is when you go back to zero and your cells reach beyond the speed of light. Once you get to the non-solid state you will be able to appear and disappear. It's very hard to believe but it has been done before.

When Parcival found the Holy Grail he disappeared. Ding! Within five years there will be many tens of thousands who will have had that experience. At the time of writing, I have seen 15 of those who were close to me, partially and/or totally disappear. The secret is very simple and it's in this book.

Once you see that your life is not solid, you can give away being you and what you think you know, and the Gladiators will come and get you. It's either one of the inner ones from another dimension, or one of the human ones. The system is so perfect; no one ever gets left out. They never miss anyone, ever. It's their dedication. Anyway, they are only inches away. All eternity is within arms length, which is hard to comprehend. Of course, you have to be in the divine plan minute by minute, or it will never be able to give you instructions to follow. You'd use your mind to override them.

God's Gladiators have four main qualities: they are very strong and brave; they are very sacred and humble;

within their humility is an absolute selflessness; and they are all heart and compassion. Their etheric speed of perception is blistering, and they are very silent. Who chose them? They chose themselves. How did they qualify? Decades of dedication, I'd imagine. You need their qualities.

Next you need to have a very solid nostalgia for eternity. One that is so strong, you are prepared to lose yourself to find that eternity. Then you have to adore God, even if you are perhaps only adoring the orange football for the moment. That's fine. Next you have to embrace humanity. That is, step forward, hold them, and love them no matter how creepy they might be. Most can never reach a true spirituality as they are distanced from humanity by their mind's obsession or revulsion with self, which shows through as hatred and disdain for other people.

Next, adore nature and call on the animals to surround you. You need their protection—without that I'm not sure what might happen. Listen to everything and watch everything. The universe talks to you via dreams, visions, and signs. It's talking and leading you along. Try to develop blind faith and trust, for you will need that, as well as endless patience.

Next, let go. Each day find one more thing to drop off at the great bus stop of life. Let no one distract you. Have a good time as you trot along, I did.

Next, listen to what your feelings are trying to tell you and do what you are told, right now immediately. Don't stall, don't dither, and don't argue. Follow orders from within right now and in their entirety. That is vital. You will never escape if you can't follow an order instantly, no matter how inconvenient.

Doing this, you develop a very strong sense of self. One that is not egotistical or brash, but silent, humble, and solid. It knows its life is not its own. It does not care. It gave itself away a long time ago.

Next, realize you can't take anyone with you. Each has to make the journey on his or her own. Keep your personal life a secret as much as feasible, given your circumstances. Say nothing. Bag romance and relationships, they will only trap you, unless your partner is highly evolved and free. If you need sex, find someone who you can love unconditionally, do what you need to do, love them, and leave.

When you are scared, raise your hands and say, "I'm scared. Love me, God, love me." Insist on God's love. Alternatively, put your hands on a tree, they act as telephone poles to God. Place your hands on the trunk, above your head, and send the energy from your root chakra up through your body via the crown chakra to the tree, then say, "Love me, God, love me." That will comfort you.

Next, insist people love you and offer them the same unconditional love. If you stuff up then say, "Sorry,

sorry, love me, love me." Don't get hung up with remorse and guilt. Remember, you have to forgive yourself to save yourself.

Also, please note that the transdimensionals track you via the resonance your voice makes on that part of your skull that is over the frontal lobe of the brain. When you move in silence, they can't find you.

Pray.

If you bump into anyone who needs help, help them at no charge. That doesn't mean you have to do everything for free, as you might have to earn money to keep things stable. But do most of your work for free. Money will come from strange places.

Last, have faith that the world will resolve itself. It will change but it won't end. Help is at hand—trust. If you get hung up on emotion, you are seeing it all short-term, not long-term. In the end, the vice like grip of these people and their nefarious ways will break open and more and more people will see the kingdom of the real God within, and when they do our world will gradually recover and save itself.

The Goddess is about to show up big time, if she has not already arrived by the time you read this. She will hurt the male, ego-dominated world, fatally wounding it. The pain will be global. The dark ones will get very scared. I imagine the light ones will also get scared at first. Then they will demand to see her beauty, or maybe she will show them anyway and become their salvation, their inspiration. It's all going to change.

Thanks for getting to here, rough ride probably—sorry, sorry, love me, love me. I've got to stop here, as there is a lot I can't mention—you'll have to work it out yourself. This is as far as I can take you. The divine plan is secret. No human on Earth knows it, for if he did he could alter or change it. I don't know it either. I don't know what I'll be doing 20 minutes from now. The idea of a human 'in the know' is drivel. The Heartland is hidden. It has to be. I'm glad of that. I'd hate any responsibility for it. I adore God and I'll help anyone I meet make a run for it if I can. But I never want to see the plan. I'm happy flying blind inside my inconsequential little world. I am not here to change anything. I'm here to offer you a freeway out, and stop thinking, wondering, and worrying. If you make a substantial move toward the exit, the Gladiators will come for you. Trust me. I'd stake my life on that. I've seen it over and over, and I've seen them. They are magnificent beyond words. They are the personification of God, though they don't know it.

In the end, if I stay with my inner messages and I don't get lost, the Gladiators will carry me out. When that happens people who know me will wonder where I went. Of course, I won't be more than a yard away, but they won't see. Remember, eternity is no further than an arm's length away. You are eternity. If the Gladiators don't get me out, or if I don't leave of my own accord, or if I make a mistake, I'll continue looking for an exit in the spirit world. There are a lot of souls there that need a chance to flee the trap they find themselves in.

I will probably never meet you, but as I said in my last book, "Let me pray for your protection from afar."

Deep love and sweet runnings,
Stuie Wilde
February 21st 2001

P.S. No one knows how many eventually got out, as when they did, they dematerialized and disappeared. Though some did come back for their own reasons.